YOUR GRANDCHILD AND YOU

ROSEMARY WELLS grew up in Scotland and England, and settled in Africa when she married. Returning to England, she was widowed and left with young children. She is a former teacher, and still enjoys teaching writers' workshops, but she is now a professional writer. Her two previous books for Sheldon Press are *Helping Children Cope with Grief* (1988) and *Helping Children Cope with Divorce* (1989).

Overcoming Common Problems Series

Beating Job Burnout
DR DONALD SCOTT

Beating the Blues
SUSAN TANNER AND JILLIAN
BALL

Being the Boss
STEPHEN FITZSIMON

Birth Over Thirty
SHEILA KITZINGER

Body Language
How to read others' thoughts by their
gestures
ALLAN PEASE

Bodypower
DR VERNON COLEMAN

Bodysense
DR VERNON COLEMAN

Calm Down
How to cope with frustration and anger
DR PAUL HAUCK

Comfort for Depression
JANET HORWOOD

Common Childhood Illnesses
DR PATRICIA GILBERT

Complete Public Speaker
GYLES BRANDRETH

**Coping Successfully with Your Child's
Asthma**
DR PAUL CARSON

**Coping Successfully with Your Child's Skin
Problems**
DR PAUL CARSON

**Coping Successfully with Your Hyperactive
Child**
DR PAUL CARSON

**Coping Successfully with Your Irritable
Bowel**
ROSEMARY NICOL

Coping with Anxiety and Depression
SHIRLEY TRICKETT

Coping with Cot Death
SARAH MURPHY

Coping with Depression and Elation
DR PATRICK McKEON

Coping with Stress
DR GEORGIA WITKIN-LANOIL

Coping with Suicide
DR DONALD SCOTT

Coping with Thrush
CAROLINE CLAYTON

Curing Arthritis – The Drug-Free Way
MARGARET HILLS

Curing Arthritis Diet Book
MARGARET HILLS

**Curing Coughs, Colds and Flu – The
Drug-Free Way**
MARGARET HILLS

Curing Illness – The Drug-Free Way
MARGARET HILLS

Depression
DR PAUL HAUCK

Divorce and Separation
ANGELA WILLANS

The Dr Moerman Cancer Diet
RUTH JOCHEMS

The Epilepsy Handbook
SHELAGH McGOVERN

**Everything You Need to Know about
Adoption**
MAGGIE JONES

**Everything You Need to Know about
Contact Lenses**
DR ROBERT YOUNGSON

**Everything You Need to Know about
Osteoporosis**
ROSEMARY NICOL

Everything You Need to Know about Shingles
DR ROBERT YOUNGSON

**Everything You Need to Know about Your
Eyes**
DR ROBERT YOUNGSON

Family First Aid and Emergency Handbook
DR ANDREW STANWAY

Overcoming Common Problems Series

Overcoming Common Problems Series

Living Alone – A Woman's Guide
LIZ McNEILL TAYLOR

Living Through Personal Crisis
ANN KAISER STEARNS

Living with Grief
DR TONY LAKE

Living with High Blood Pressure
DR TOM SMITH

Loneliness
DR TONY LAKE

Making Marriage Work
DR PAUL HAUCK

Making the Most of Loving
GILL COX AND SHEILA DAINOW

Making the Most of Yourself
GILL COX AND SHEILA DAINOW

Managing Two Careers
How to survive as a working mother
PATRICIA O'BRIEN

Meeting People is Fun
How to overcome shyness
DR PHYLLIS SHAW

Menopause
RAEWYN MACKENZIE

The Nervous Person's Companion
DR KENNETH HAMBLY

Overcoming Fears and Phobias
DR TONY WHITEHEAD

Overcoming Shyness
A woman's guide
DIANNE DOUBTFIRE

Overcoming Stress
DR VERNON COLEMAN

Overcoming Tension
DR KENNETH HAMBLY

Overcoming Your Nerves
DR TONY LAKE

The Parkinson's Disease Handbook
DR RICHARD GODWIN-AUSTEN

Say When!
Everything a woman needs to know about
alcohol and drinking problems
ROSEMARY KENT

Self-Help for your Arthritis
EDNA PEMBLE

Sleep Like a Dream – The Drug-Free Way
ROSEMARY NICOL

Solving your Personal Problems
PETER HONEY

Someone to Love
How to find romance in the personal columns
MARGARET NELSON

A Special Child in the Family
Living with your sick or disabled child
DIANA KIMPTON

Stress and your Stomach
DR VERNON COLEMAN

Think Your Way to Happiness
DR WINDY DRYDEN AND JACK GORDON

Trying to Have a Baby?
Overcoming infertility and child loss
MAGGIE JONES

What Everyone Should Know about Drugs
KENNETH LEECH

Why Be Afraid?
How to overcome your fears
DR PAUL HAUCK

Women and Depression
A practical self-help guide
DEIDRE SANDERS

You and Your Varicose Veins
DR PATRICIA GILBERT

Your Arthritic Hip and You
GEORGE TARGET

Overcoming Common Problems

YOUR GRANDCHILD
AND YOU

Rosemary Wells

SHELDON PRESS
LONDON

First published in Great Britain 1990
Sheldon Press, SPCK, Marylebone Road, London NW1 4DU

British Library Cataloguing in Publication Data

Wells, Rosemary
    Your grandchild and you. – (Overcoming common problems)
    I. Title   II. Series
    306.87

    ISBN 0–85969–618–9

Typeset by Deltatype Ltd, Ellesmere Port S. Wirral
Printed in Great Britain by Courier International Ltd, Tiptree, Essex

Contents

Acknowledgements

I am indebted to many, many grandparents and grandchildren for ideas, comments and discussions shared with me during the writing of this book. I thank them all sincerely.

I would also like to thank the several grandparents' organizations, legal centres, elderly persons' homes, retirement associations, schools and universities, youth clubs, church groups, and various family institutions – all of whom have given generous information and advice.

My gratitude also goes to the teachers, doctors, social workers and counsellors who gave of their time, expertise and support. I cannot mention all their names, but a few must be singled out for special thanks: Jo Clay and Noreen Tingle of the Grandparents' Federation; Jo Tunnard of the Family Rights Group; Nigel Lowe of Bristol University; and not least Mr Ray Powell, MP, who kept me up-to-date with the Readings of the Children Bill.

1

Grandparents Today and Yesterday

Here we are, rocketed into the next generation,
without so much as a by-your-leave!

Jim and Susan, both 45 years old, expressed ambivalent emotions when presented with the news of their first grandchild. This feeling of being brushed prematurely into old age is understandable. As one glamorous actress in her early forties says: 'I'm thrilled my daughter is having a baby, but I refuse to be called granny.'

Most parents are at least half way through their allotted lifespans when they become grandparents. So their new label has an immediate image of white hair, possibly a walking stick, and is slotted into the category of *the older generation*, despite the fact that in Britain today the average age of a first-time grandparent is around 47 years.

Victorian grandparents

Would we have heard such comments a century ago? Grandparents were perhaps younger than they are today – at the turn of the century life expectancy was 48 years for men and 52 for women – the parenting and grandparenting took place much earlier. Yet grandfather would be the undeniable patriarch – with side whiskers, a watch-chain gleaming over his increasing stomach, and an air of authority which his many grandchildren never dared to dispute. Grandmother would wear her long black dresses with quiet resignation and dignity, and know that her role as the bustling heart of the family was to be exchanged for that of the *old lady* sitting by the fire with her knitting.

Even my own paternal grandmother, in the 1940s, smelled of lavender water and never went shopping without her hat and gloves. We loved her, but never expected her to play tennis with us, or go out to work – she was very obviously a generation older than our parents.

Mr R, who has been a grandfather for nearly thirty years, recalls his grandfather in 1908:

He was very strict, never let us talk at meals and yet he did not punish us as my father used to. If we ran errands for him he would give us a penny each. I thought he must be very rich, as father never gave us more than a halfpenny.

Mrs S, now over 100 years old, has clear memories of *her* grandparents at the turn of the century: 'Grandmother smoked a clay pipe and wore long dark skirts, buttoned boots and high lace collars.' She still recalls the hard work all this involved:

Oh dear, the endless labour. Grandmama had a young girl in to do the washing one day a week, she couldn't have been more than thirteen, and it took all day – twelve hours of scrubbing on a ridged board in the scullery. Then Grandmama did the ironing herself – all that crimping with a goffering iron on the lace trimmings and collars.

I asked Mrs S if her grandmother was very strict:

She insisted we knew the ten commandments by heart, and sent us to bed if we forgot even one, but we loved her. She would give me and my sisters a petticoat each for Christmas, a great treat. Most of our presents would be handkerchiefs or packets of sweets.

Victorian grandmothers slipped easily into their new roles. Never long without a baby on their laps, they cradled the grandchildren as they came along, sometimes at the same time as their own youngest children.

Father was always rather a mysterious figure to his own children, to whom he appeared each morning for prayers and each evening for 'conversation with papa'. He hardly noticed when the youngsters who were presented to him, washed and dressed in formal clothes, were whispering 'Good evening *grand*papa' and not 'papa', as they made their bows and curtsies.

Yet they are mostly pleasant memories, some exceptionally warm and happy:

> Grandma was always sitting in her rocking chair in the kitchen, next to the range, when we came home from school. Mama threatened us with no tea if we did not finish our homework before papa came in, but grandma always gave us a mug of tea and a thick slice of bread and jam. She seemed to be *on our side*.

Megan remembers her childhood on a Welsh farm in 1919:

> Ours was a large family – uncles and aunts and lots of children. Mum was always busy with babies and washing and cooking, and we never knew if mum or aunty would help us dress. Da was up at daybreak to tend lambs or walk to market. Grandfather was the only adult really able to *listen* to us children. He would tell us stories too, of when his da bought the farm and the year they were snowed in and a baby died of colic before they could dig their way out. We loved his old tales, the more dramatic the better!

Scattered families

Megan, now a great-grandmother, is sorry for today's children. 'They don't have grandparents like we had, always available, ready to listen. Some of them live hundreds of miles away – what's the use of that?'

She is right. Many families have grandchildren spread around the world, let alone being miles apart in this country. Grandparents can be, and often are, an enormous source of strength for their families. They provide a sense of connection and continuation – very exciting once recognized by grandparents and grandchildren alike.

Young Rupert seems to be taking after grandpa – look at his aptitude for mathematics.

Grandmama used to play the piano like me!

Today, at the start of the 1990s, 15 per cent of the population in Britain are over 65, and with life expectancy at 72 years for men and 77 years for women, there should be many years for us all to share with our grandchildren if not great-grandchildren.

'I feel we have a lot to offer our families as well as society,' says Mr B, who has been active in voluntary work for nine years. His grandson confirms his views: 'Grandfather has been my greatest encouragement in my career. His tips for commercial and social behaviour are invaluable. Whoever says grandparents are old-fashioned is plain ignorant – nothing can replace experience.'

A grandmother of 90 agrees: 'Old-fashioned is an absurd label for those of us who are the same age as the century. Consider the changes we've seen – from horsedrawn carriages to Concorde, and men on the moon!'

Grandparents today are having to take on board amazing innovations, and most of them do so with astonishing calm. One friend of 85 pointed out that fashions in behaviour have made the most dramatic of alterations:

My granddaughter was staying with me and as I'm always the first awake I took her some early morning tea – to find her in bed with her boyfriend. I survived the shock, but spoke to her later – rather seriously – about the consequences of her actions. 'But Gran, he's my friend, nothing happened!' she said calmly. I can only say that young men must have changed very much since my young days if that was true.

Not all grandparents, of course, are the ever-charming, all-understanding paragons of the family. Grandparents cannot be categorized any more than uncles, aunts, cousins, or teenagers – they are not a readily labelled breed. They do not, and hopefully will never, conform to a pattern. Grandparenthood does not automatically confer loving natures or sweet tempers, or even a sense of humour on those fortunate enough to reach that status.

The honour is bestowed on many who, according to their relations, do not deserve it. Irascible old ladies, and fussy old gentlemen do not change by being pushed up a generation – they often become increasingly irritable and a 'pain in the neck' for their families. Even when tragedy strikes or squabbles arise, grandparents are not always helpful; they can sometimes, as we shall see in later chapters, be the *cause* of family disputes, and exacerbate rifts in relationships.

Not all families are happy. But even when parent–child relationships have been strained, if not untenable, the two-generation gap often works wonderfully well. Because of this, it would seem that in the majority of families, grandparents are an increasingly tolerant, valuable asset for those lucky enough to have them around.

> We are a volatile family, with as many ups and downs as there are days in the week – but granny and grandpa are there in the background with their unconditional love for us all – they are fantastic. I wish the grandchildren were as flexible in *their* attitudes.

Ageism

The whole subject of ageism is to do with *attitudes*, isn't it? Our own, our children's, and those of anyone older than ourselves.

Ageing is a process that begins at birth, so how does it become the dreaded, almost taboo topic as soon as we reach adulthood? Many youngsters, and their middle-aged parents, tend to dismiss the aged, or the elderly, as a race apart from themselves. But as a general rule, the over-sixties belie their political image of 'useless old folk with deteriorating bodies and declining minds'.

I feel there is something very encouraging, very exciting, in the new image the 1990s generation of grandparents is presenting. They are at last wanting to make society understand that they are *not* a different species once they have passed into and beyond middle-age. The obsession with ageism in the western world is perhaps at last being eroded – certainly laughed at – by today's grandparents, and of course I am talking here of those well over retirement age.

Have you noticed that it is seldom the elderly themselves who talk about being old, or stress the awfulness of reaching three-score years and ten, or the shame and dread that turn old age into a disease? One researcher expressed well the feelings of many grandparents: 'Old age is not a condition, such images should be exorcised, and exorcised fast, and for ever.' An actress, well into her seventies and still working, said if she were a fairy godmother she would see to it that when a person is given a pension book, they are not treated as an idiot who is 'deaf, daft and unable to do or understand anything'. There are hundreds of examples of famous octogenarians who are achieving success in every sphere of life – actors and actresses, diplomats and politicians, novelists, film directors, musicians and business consultants – and scores of not-so-famous but admirable grand-parents who are enjoying their *third age* to the full.

As on all subjects – opinions, even professional ones, are divided. 'Age is a privilege,' is countered by 'No, it is a punishment.' For those whose health, especially mental health, fails drastically with the years, it does indeed seem a cruel punishment in the last decades of life. 'Just as we need our faculties they are taken from us,' grumbled an 87-year-old. But for those whose 'ageing' is only apparent in a few grey hairs, some extra wrinkles, and some 'freckles' on their hands – it is surely a privilege. To quote several personalities who have used the phrase in their later years: 'Consider the alternative!'

In the first half of our lives we tend to think that when old the senses will dim and interest in living decline and gradually cease. On the contrary, many people's senses appear to sharpen, their interest in life quickens, and their enthusiasm for anything new remains as lively as it was in their teens.

Joan is in her late seventies, a small round, loveable gran with an arthritic hip and a hearing aid. Her twin grandsons of sixteen think she is 'Amazingly good fun!' But Joan laughs at them. 'It's not amazing at all. Inside this rolypoly old lady I'm still *me*, somewhere around 50, going on 25!'

Talking with the grandchildren

Author Ronald Blythe hit upon a universal truth when he wrote:

> The most pleasurable and rewarding relationship in old age is that with young grandchildren, prepubertal boys and girls, with all of whom the grandparent can enter into a rich conspiracy of stories, embraces, secrets, bribes, teasing, and even sly battles mounted against mother, school, etc.

Conversations with your grandchildren are a great way to combat the western world's absurd obsession with ageism, and to suppress the patronizing tones used when speaking to and of the older generation. Last week I saw a great-grandmother in jeans and she looked a lot neater in them than her overplump granddaughter did in hers. Yet it was poor great-gran who was criticized: 'Fancy dressing like that *at your age.*'

If you ask children about *old* people, they seldom include their own grandparents, unless they are in hospital or residential homes. Even then, they are gran or grandad – not one of the *oldies* they hear discussed on TV as being in need of charity, or hidden away in an institution.

Age discrimination

Not that it is only elderly folk who are discriminated against on the grounds of age. Age has become a dominant factor in every phase of life – it is even a handicap at school if your birthday falls in the wrong year!

Somehow the word *age* has become synonymous with the word *old* in the English language. We ask 'How *old* are you?' and not 'What *age* are you?'

It is going to take government help to emphasize the need for strict adherence to anti-ageism policies in all areas of life: education, work and leisure activities. How sad that legislation has become the only way to bring about what should be a natural attitude.

In the meantime, worrying signs have appeared on several new housing developments, such as 'For the over-fifty-fives.' Why should reaching such an age, any age, cause men and women to be treated as though they have to be segregated from the rest of society? They may well have more than a third of their lives yet to live, and live them they intend to, not go into an isolated decline. It is good to see children, parents, newly married couples, grandparents, all living in the same neighbourhood. Watch any group of mothers waiting for the children coming out of primary school – all in casual clothes, mostly track suits – and as one teacher says: 'You never know if it's a mum or a gran fetching the kids.'

Think of a world with only 40-year-olds, or only 70–year-olds. What a dreary place would result.

A grandmother sold her flat and went to live in a retirement home, but after a year came out again. She had nowhere to live, had sold all her belongings, but with the help of friends she started again. I asked why the change of heart and she answered: 'My dear, all the people there were old.'

A spokesperson from *Help the Aged* organization feels that we are still 'a deeply ageist society, and all carry with us negative expectations of dependency, that is, if you are active and busy, you are not old. I think we have a long way to go before we get rid of those attitudes.'

A retired solicitor, now in her eighties, who has thirteen grandchildren all of whom adore her, agrees wholeheartedly that being treated as a 'write-off' due to age is just not to be tolerated. She was suffering from a swollen, painful right leg and on showing it to her doctor he said, in a soothing voice as though talking to a small child: 'You must be patient, Mrs M, there is not much else to do, at your age.' To which she replied: 'My left leg is not swollen and it is exactly the same age as the right one.' Grudgingly, that doctor admitted her to hospital, and cured her complaint. It was not her doctor's incompetence, merely his *attitude*, that was at fault.

'Old Pat'

One of the best research projects (and the most revealing) into such attitudes was carried out in America by a girl in her twenties. She disguised herself as 'Old Pat' and tramped the streets of over 100 cities, including New York, for three years – at times alternating the frail, elderly image with that of her own agile and attractive self. Attitudes changed immediately.

As 'Old Pat' she met with verbal abuse, aggressive behaviour, even assault, and so much condescending behaviour that she found herself intimidated and self-effacing. She proved that it *is* these attitudes, and *not* the many physical disabilities that the elderly are prone to, that cause such unhappiness. At times she felt guilty that she could drop her disguise and return to a youthful body when she wished – but was told by many of the genuinely elderly people she confided in: 'But *we* feel the same as you – we too have young minds trapped behind old faces.'

Her happiest experience was when she met a six-year-old boy who chatted to her as a friend, an equal. 'That child,' she says, 'didn't know any better.' He had not been brainwashed, as we all are daily, by society, the media, the advertisers, the unthinking.

Positive thinking

We have to start to think positively about this, and appreciate that there are no elderly people, only people older than ourselves. We are all guilty, or have been at some time in our lives, of looking on older people as objects of pity. We should all be sympathetic where age has brought disability or deprivation, but as Alison Norman, internationally known for her work in the field of social gerontology, has written:

The word *old* is itself felt to be insulting when used to describe people, so we employ euphemisms such as *pensioner* and *senior citizen*. *Senile*, *crumbly*, *gaga* are overtly derogatory, but still worse is the common use of *geriatric* as a noun to describe a frail old person instead of its correct use as the branch of medical science concerned with old people and their illnesses. We do not call a woman who has had a hysterectomy 'an obstetric' or a sick child 'a paediatric'.

Caring for elderly people is a profession held in low esteem, and to care for one's grandparents is often done out of a sense of duty, with a patronizing attitude – so hurtful to a loving grandparent.

Linking grandparents and grandchildren

Among the young many of these attitudes are beginning to drop away as they see for themselves that grandparents can be active and interesting, and many children are feeling respect – even admiration – for their elders. In Britain, an organization aptly named *Link Age*, is successfully managing to develop and strengthen such attitudes. It is a charitable trust set up originally to carry out research on issues such as discrimination against grandparents of children in care, and the effects of public policy and practice on the extended family. It also runs schemes promoting links between grandparent and grandchild generations. These go beyond the familiar 'singing to the old folk' that many schools arrange at Christmas. Some schools invite residents from nursing homes or sheltered housing communities to school dinners. Grandpa John, as he is affectionately known to the children in a primary school, is a great favourite at table. 'He loves baked beans and always asks for seconds. He tells us about his school where he used to get beaten with a cane!'

One of the Link Age organizers in a North London community has helped one school to liaise with elderly long-stay patients in the local hospital. With the help of the hospital voluntary services organizer, and the cooperation of the class teacher, she arranges a different project each week. First, she gave talks on old age – what it means, how people feel, how they are treated.

We tell them to face an elderly person when talking; we tell them elderly people like to be taken by the hand, and that hand may be bent, or bony; we explain that they like to hear about the world outside hospital, but also to talk about their own childhood.

I walked with a class of eight-year-olds and their teacher for an afternoon at the hospital. Several of the children told me the name of the patient they had made friends with, and they rushed off to help the nurses fetch them in wheelchairs from the wards. That day they were making sweets – a sticky but colourful operation –with helpful advice and enthusiastic tasting from the grandparents!

The hospital director told me that many of the patients are listless, seldom eating very much – but on days when the children arrive, they brighten up and find their appetites: 'It is wonderful the difference these children have made to our patients' lives.'

The children too have learned a great deal. Many of their parents are reluctant to be drawn in to help, but at least the youngsters are growing up with a better, and caring, understanding of what 'growing old' means.

Grandparents heading for the 21st century

Not to be forgotten, and several over-eighties have impressed this view upon me, there is an important group of people in our society who can do something positive to change this ageist outlook – the older generation themselves. The over-retirement age grandparents, and great-grandparents, need to show by their own vigour and enthusiasm how ageism in relation to those over fifty is totally irrelevant and unnecessary.

In the USA 'the grey lobby' has a powerful voice and has been responsible for radical changes in legislation regarding discrimination, pensions and healthcare. In Britain, a similar campaign is under way. The strong voices of the grandparent generation are being heard as they grow in number and realize the potential of harnessing their economic and social strengths. By their determination to continue and enjoy their usefulness in the community, they are greatly enhancing the quality and purpose of their lives.

Future generations of grandparents will have much to thank these first 'third agers' for, as they live out their final two or three decades to the full, well into the next century.

2

Grandmothers

MOTHER TO DAUGHTER (FOR CATHERINE)
> *Your pain*
> *I could not bear for you.*
> *I could not remember*
> *my pain for you.*
> *Only the small life in my arms –*
> *My girl, my daughter – you.*
>   Barbara Rennie

It needs a poet to express the emotions many grandmothers feel on the birth of their grandchildren.

> Every time I think of the little creatures my heart gives a jump.

> When my son phoned me in the middle of the night with the news, I lay back in bed and couldn't stop smiling.

There will be a wealth of emotions: some grandmothers who have reluctantly put away the prams and cots after their own last child, and have mourned as one by one their babes left the nest, will exalt in the thought of nurseries and nappies again and be longing to become part of the new family's life. Others, who parted with nursery trappings with thankfulness, and rejoiced when left with an orderly household as the teenagers finally left home, will still feel intense pleasure.

> Wonderful! I can *enjoy* this new generation, without having to cope with any of the mess.

Graceful or disgraceful?

There are two definite theories amongst women approaching grandparenthood: (a) those who firmly refute the idea that on reaching the new status (at whatever age from 30 to 70) they must begin to change or disguise their personalities; and (b) those who long to be 'a real granny'.

The author Penelope Mortimer is among the first, and seemingly growing number of grandmothers determined to 'grow old disgracefully' as distinct from trying to stay young. 'God forbid,' she says. 'If I dance, scream on the Big Dipper, paddle in rock pools, chew gum, jump off diving boards holding my nose . . . it will be because I *want* to.' And is there a grandmother who could argue with such sound reasoning?

But it is hard not to sympathize with those other grandmothers, most of them still working and with not a grey hair between them, who feel rather disillusioned with their new status. One recently retired nurse sounded wistful as she told me of her secret longing for a rocking chair in a warm kitchen and a cat on her lap – enchanting and adoring grandchildren at her feet: 'My husband is allowed to play grandpa with his long abandoned waistline and shaggy white beard. But I'm expected to join the over-sixties keep fit and dance class and eat yogurt for breakfast – it's not fair!'

One septuagenarian granny is also feeling cheated out of her 'cosy gran' image.

After years of hard work, I want to relax – not necessarily in a rocker on my back porch – but I refuse to diet myself into a Joan Collins or exercise my limbs along with Jane Fonda, or learn to fly helicopters. I want to enjoy being a *real* granny, like my own darling nana was.

'Paperback granny'

It is good to hear such 'nanas' talking. So often nowadays granny is not around to turn to for advice. 'Are those spots measles or chickenpox?' 'What do I do if he won't drink his milk?'

One young mother told me she bought the well-known Dr Spock baby book. 'I called it my paperback Granny,' she said, 'turning to it as I would have turned to my mother had she been around.'

A lifeline

If you know a 'Granny-less' family, in particular one with a single mother trying to cope – perhaps you could try to pair them up with a 'grandchildless' parent (see Chapter 5). Or, find out if there is a *Newpin* group in their neighbourhood. This is a self-help organization which incorporates counselling as well as companionship for lonely and/or depressed mothers. For I feel grandmothers could be of enormous help – not only in passing on their old tried and tested hints – but in keeping up to date with current sources of help and information for young families far too busy to search them out for themselves. Newpin could virtually save the sanity of an otherwise isolated family, perhaps in a large and impersonal city (see 'Sources of Help and Information').

Healing the rifts

I have often heard mothers say that on the arrival of a baby their daughters become much closer to them emotionally: 'Patsy never confided in me since she was about fourteen, and now the baby has come she pours it all out, it is as though we are sisters. And she lets me share the baby, it is such a joy.'

A new grandchild, born to a daughter, often results in the healing of a rift between a mother and daughter who may have had differences, or simply not had any close rapport for many years. Tearful arguments have perhaps occurred during the rebellious teenage years, or on marriage to a partner the mother disapproves of, or due to a choice of career which is alien to a mother's way of life. Then a baby appears and suddenly the daughter is thrown into the role of mother – the two women are on the same wavelength at last.

Difficulties ahead

Not every birth creates such family bonds – all is not always sweetness and light. There are grandmothers who live miles, even continents, away from their daughters; there are others who live far too close. Not all young couples are able to afford a home of their own, even a room, and have to live with their parents. This is not easy, and once babies come along, can become claustrophobic. Grandmother may complain, criticize and refuse even to babysit; she may become the dreaded interferer who expects to mother her daughter and grandchild together; daughter or daughter-in-law may become hostile to a grandmother who seems to be denying her any independence. Some young mums appear to use a baby to 'get back at' a mother-in-law, or mother, whom they see as a rival – sometimes with tragic consequences (see Chapter 7).

Conversely, many grandmothers become obsessed with jealousy, perhaps accusing a new mother of gross incompetence, gradually undermining the marriage. 'You never come to see me any more, it's always the children coming first.'

It may be that such words are spoken by widowed or divorced grandmothers who pour all their energies and emotions into their grandchildren. Understandably, they are seeking love from their families, but their behaviour often alienates young parents. Many of these lonely grandmothers do not realize until too late that they have first to find fulfilment in an independent life, before they are able to offer truly balanced love to their families. So sad, when a loving grandfather could have helped to smooth the atmosphere in the household.

An assertive young mother, perhaps used to living in a large family, might cope well with such a situation, but many grow resentful and a young husband is often blackmailed into breaking all ties with his mother.

Other young mothers take advantage of an over-willing grandmother; she finds herself constantly sitting-in, doing all the tedious jobs and having little time to enjoy the children and babies. But a grandmother has also to remember that it is not fair to go against the rules of discipline the young parents decide on.

Her role can be an extremely helpful one for grandchildren. It often happens that one child in a family tends to be left out – to be quiet, shy, perhaps not so bright as the others. Grandmothers usually spot this while mum is too busy to notice, and can give some special time and attention to the 'loner'. She can encourage a hidden talent, and perhaps give that child a much-needed dollop of praise and confidence – an extra dose of granny-love.

Meanwhile, grandmother must not forget that she has a counterpart – will she be friend or rival? Absurd jealousies can creep in to what is often a tenuous relationship. 'Your son never was good enough for my daughter!' The author Jilly Cooper once described the situation as *granny-mosity*, which conjured up a superb picture of two grans currying favour of wickedly knowing grandchildren. 'Let's see if grandma or nana brings the most chocolates this week!'

Most families are able to sort out their problems – most grandmothers are loving and beloved, their role is an enviable one. But for any families where relationships are strained and there is danger of serious estrangement, especially for the grandchildren, I do advise seeking experienced help. If you know of a family who are ignorant that help for families exists (and many people are reticent to call in outsiders to sort their intimate differences) do try to persuade them to 'give it a try'. Families *do* matter.

Dr Mia Pringle, one of the most caring of child psychiatrists, once wrote: 'The quality of family relationships is of basic importance to a child's psychological development.'

The National Family Trust

In Britain, this Trust is a non-political, charitable organization working to promote and defend the interest of families. How sad that such groups have to campaign for what should be a natural order of life in a civilized society, but they are right when they say that family life today is under threat in many ways. Sir Harry Secombe, one of their patrons, writes:

The best gift we can have, or give our children, is a stable, caring and loving family and a secure home to live in. Not that such families don't have problems, but at least they contain a shared commitment to solving whatever difficulties arise among their members, come what may.

More often than not it is because family members do not talk to each other enough that misunderstandings arise and then grow into really serious differences. Family counsellors, therapists, and *Relate* marriage guidance are all available to help families open discussions; it is surprising how families start to listen to each other when there is a neutral third party sitting with them. Try to point out to your family that it is *not* a sign of failure, of being unable to cope, if they seek outside help. It is a sign of caring concern.

One grandmother contacted an organization called *The Parent Network*, which was launched in 1986 'to fill a serious gap in the provision of education for parenthood by establishing a national network of parent support groups'. She was delighted to find that parent does include grandparent, or any other adult caring for children. *Parent-Link* is a continuing programme of this organization, whose philosophy is based on a person-centred approach. It is much more about prevention than a cure for serious individual or family problems. Any family with special needs is referred to other sources of help, as grandmother Joan found:

> I was very concerned that my grandchildren were being brought up in a tense, acrimonious household, but they would never let me help. It took tactful persuasion to get my son and his wife to attend a Parent-Link session; they were both hostile to any of my suggestions. I also attended, and saw that by trying to impose my theories for bringing up children I had increased my son's guilt at not being a better parent. That was six months ago, and last weekend they asked me to stay. We have all learned so much about relationships – the whole family has relaxed.

The 'granny bore'

Two grandmothers met for lunch. Towards the end of the meal one said: 'Do you realize I haven't mentioned my grandchildren all through the meal?' To which her friend replied: 'Thank you dear, I'm very grateful.' We all know the grandmother bore – when pride gets out of hand the other generations are embarrassed.

But that is only one of the pitfalls for grandmothers to avoid. For along with the overwhelming pleasures of grandchildren come equally overwhelming temptations which have to be resisted if you want to remain on friendly terms with the rest of the family.

Brenda's second grandson has just arrived and she cannot understand why her daughter has not asked her to babysit as she did the time before. Her daughter explained: 'Mother changed overnight from a good friend into a critical, bossy, interfering woman. She seems to think being the grandmother gives her the right to tell me, and my husband, how to look after a baby.'

I have heard such grannies – proud as anything of the new babies – but totally without sympathy for the young mothers. 'Postnatal depression? What nonsense! Never heard of it in *my* day. We just had a good cry then jolly well got on with it!'

It is not, however, simply a matter of another generation. Gran's ideas may be out of date (demand feeding may be out, bottle feeding may be in or vice versa) – it is also the understanding that every mother uses her own instincts as to what is best for her baby. As one granny wisely remarked:

> Young parents today appear to have it all, but there are widely different and conflicting ideas and philosophies handed out to them from all directions. There are no rigid guidelines any more, so it's up to each mother's own common sense. She will need to be supported, not criticized, in her decisions.

First baby

This is an anxious time for a young girl. If baby cries she feels he must be ill; if he sleeps she listens every ten minutes to see if he's still breathing. It is a huge responsibility she has never known before, and if granny is standing over criticizing every move, it is sometimes a stress that causes real breakdown.

But I never bathed *you* in the afternoon, darling.
I don't think it's sensible to give baby a bottle *before* you feed him.

If you are a first-time grandmother, you will have to hold back such comments – this baby is not yours. All right, it is difficult for experienced grandmothers to stand by and watch a young mum struggling to hold a slippery baby in his first bath; to listen to a baby's screams as an ill-fitting teat is held at an awkward angle for his tiny mouth. Just grit your teeth, sit down and recall *your* first baby. How many mistakes did you make? If asked for help or advice, that is different, but even then a tactful 'You're so clever at these modern nappies, dear,' is a better opening to your suggestions than 'Well, of course, if you *must* put him in those ridiculous clothes . . .'

It is the same old story – be available, but not *so* available that you are in the way.

The reluctant granny

So you are young, still working, with little time to bother with grandchildren, and no desire to be hugged with sticky fingers or kissed by jammy lips? Besides, you never were enchanted with tiny babies: 'I didn't enjoy my own until they could walk and talk, so why should I be thrilled with my son's offspring?'

Rather than interfering, that gran is seldom free to babysit, and is only happy for the children to visit her on fine days when 'they can stay in the garden'. Once they are school age she will no doubt be popular with her five grandsons. 'I'm looking forward to taking them to the cinema.'

Also reluctant to be 'shoved up a generation' are some very young parents whose daughters marry and start families immediately on leaving school.

'I'm actually looking forward to my daughter having a child,' says the still beautiful film actress Priscilla Presley. 'But I haven't been able to confront being called *that name* (grandmother).'

But she is only one among a number of attractive women today who belong – whether they admit it or not – in the ranks of grandmotherhood. Elizabeth Taylor and Joan Collins spring to mind, but there are many grandmothers of all ages who not only look glamorous, but enter competitions to prove it.

Glamorous grandmothers

It was that most famous of all grandmothers, Marlene Dietrich, who inspired Sir Billy Butlin back in the 1950s to search for glamorous grandmothers in Britain. Ever since then his Glamorous Grandmother of Great Britain contest has attracted over 10,500 entrants each year. The youngest competitor ever known was 32 years of age and the eldest 96 (one occasion when *age* is definitely relevant and worth mentioning as I'm sure you will agree – not a hint of ageism here!)

These contests cannot be accused of exploiting the female sex either. The organizers tell me that all the entrants volunteer for the enormous fun, and for the entertainment of their families. Perhaps Wendy, aged seven, had the most apt comment when her grandmother was among the final twenty: 'Nana looks just as good as a film star, *and* she makes the best chocolate brownies in our street!'

Monte Carlo Dash

And for a different sort of glamour, what about the Monte Carlo Dash? In 1988, the first Dash was made by lady car-drivers over 60 ('Well over', said several grandmothers proudly, chiding the press for calling the event 'the Granny Rally'). Each car, with driver and navigator, set off from Brands Hatch racing track, completing two circuits before making for the south of France. They spent three nights en route – and it was such a success it is now an annual event.

Jealousy

When the children are older and can communicate with their grandparents, you may find that daughters are actually jealous of the love and attention you lavish on their children. 'Mother never loved *me* like that.' Quite unconsciously, these daughters use their own children to punish their mothers for the way they feel they were treated when young. 'No, mother, today's paediatricians say you should keep babies in the home with a stable carer – you did it all wrong taking me everywhere with you.'

Poor grandma, it seems you never did anything right! I would suggest a sense of humour would see you through this type of situation. Some grandmas, however, instead of learning from the new generation, go into a decline and become embittered – losing the enjoyment of their grandchildren into the bargain. Others, like the American writer Judith Viorst's mother, appear to enjoy their grandchildren more than they enjoyed their own children – and because of this have finally made a new, happy connection between mother and daughter.

Some grandmothers feel sad, and filled with regrets:

I see now where I went wrong with my own children. I wish I could have my time again. I'm jealous of my daughter with her free and easy way of talking to her babies and all the easy-care equipment she has – disposable nappies; prams that convert into car seats; shoulder carriers for walking; ready cooked foods for travelling. Yes, I'm jealous.

But that is negative thinking – life for grandmothers should never be wasted on regrets.

The two-generation gap

The two-generation gap can create one of the best relationships within a family. Life with your school-age grandchildren, even the teenagers (a label many grandmothers never had to suffer themselves), can be enormous fun.

Listening to various family members talking of their grand-mothers surely provides an excellent case for preserving this relationship above all others:

My grandmother gave me my love of reading.

Without granny I would have had a very lonely childhood.

I have also heard very different views (see Chapter 10), but they are seldom of great significance:

I hate going to grandma's house, she's such a fusspot!

Granny is horrid – she won't let me have a puppy!

Nicholas, now in his twenties, says he remembers making such remarks when at school. But now his friendship with his 78-year-old grandmother is such that she has become his intimate confidante: 'When I told gran this girl was the one I was going to marry, she was wonderful – never questioned and doubted, or put forward endless arguments like my parents did. She welcomed Sally and gave us hope in our future together.' Lucky Nicholas, and other youngsters able to turn to a grandmother for caring yet objective advice.

If you can keep such balanced viewpoints, your grandchildren will be very appreciative. No grandparent wants to be called old-fashioned, but even a generation back is dated in the eyes of the young, and grandmothers do need to avoid recalling their own experiences when trying to advise a youngster.

Grandmother Molly regaled her only granddaughter with horror stories of the menopause. 'You keep having your curse as long as possible, my love – when it stops, life is awful!' She never intended to depress the child, but had not moved into the present day and attempted to view life through a young girl's eyes – a warning to us all.

When grandmothers are still young, some relationships become more complicated even than stepfamilies. This does not happen quite so often as it used to in Victorian times, when mothers would continue to bear children for up to twenty years – so that by the time the fourteenth or fifteenth baby arrived, the eldest daughter would be married and having children of her own. But it does still happen.

'I'm four years older than my aunty,' says Doreen, and it's not hard to work that one out. She was four years old when her grandmother, still in her thirties, had another baby. Curiously, Doreen always thought of her grandmother as 'an old lady, even though she was seldom without a baby at her breast'.

As late as the 1920s, grannies were thought of as 'the older generation' and not expected to dress in anything other than discreet, figure-hiding clothes. Tom D remembers being looked after by his grandmother in 1912:

> Mother was a weaver in a factory and went to work before sunrise. So my brothers and I were brought up by grandma. She seemed old to us, but she could not have been more than 40. She scrubbed and cleaned and cooked, I don't ever remember her sitting down. When mum came in at 5.30 for lunch, grandma went back to cook grandpa's meal. All the homes in the street were the same – I don't know what happened to families without grandmothers.

Grandmother's home of memories

I think the luckiest grandmothers are those who still live in the same homes as they were in when *their* children were born. I envy their grandchildren too. The old cots and prams are waiting in the attic, the chewed teddy bears, the battered old dolls' house. One grandmother found a pile of action men, and another a box of Dinky cars – all surprisingly welcomed by grandchildren in this day of computer games. So many of us have moved around from house to house, even from country to country, and to have kept such family heirlooms was impossible. But they do give an amazing stability, no – security – to a family: the children know that grandma's house is full of toys that mummy played with, and the crib that mummy and aunty slept in. Some still have grandfather's old rocking horse in the nursery – yes, in 1990!

Even if you have no such home of memories to offer, a granny who can pull out a drawer of photographs (even in a hospital bedside table) and show the grandchildren snapshots of their parents when at school, or on holidays, and provide pictures of the old family house – will always be popular. She will probably have time to explain who all the old relations are –their names and where they lived and what games they played and who they all married.

A young executive granny took her grandchildren round the city. Yes, they adored seeing it all, but they were equally delighted when she was able to show them a home movie of their parents on a beach holiday when they were ten years old. 'That was the *best* fun!'

So that's what grandmothering is all about

Granny Betty and young Tracey, eleven, are the best of friends. The other day her father found Tracey packing a small case and asked her where she was going. 'I'm going to granny's house. I can't stand you and mum quarrelling any more. I feel safe with granny, it's quiet so I can do my homework.'

Children do not all have quarrelling parents, though some have far from quiet homes. Grandmothers who provide a secure refuge ('I always tell the children I'm here if they want me') even just a peaceful haven away from a large family, are surely the best sort of grandmothers to have. In fact, grandmothers emerge in several recent British surveys as the most significant figures in caring for children while mothers go out to work. In 1980, grandmothers were used by 44 per cent of full-time and 24 per cent of part-time working mothers of preschool children, and they also were second only to fathers in looking after school-age children out of school hours.

In spite of, or perhaps because of, these figures, many family therapists advice grandmothers *not* to give up work to devote their whole time to new grandchildren, unless they are able to help a young family in practical ways by doing so, and only if the family are happy at the idea.

Timothy, thirteen, and his family do not live in each other's pockets, but there is obviously real trust and affection between the generations. 'I like to ring up my granny, she always cheers me up.'

This must be what being a grandmother is all about.

3
Grandfathers

It is really no problem having grandchildren. Most are returnable in the late afternoon and the house is usually tidy again by 8 o'clock.

Robert Morley

I cannot imagine the well-known actor Robert Morley being anything other than loving and lovable as a grandfather. However, his remark, as with so many witticisms, has an underlying truth. Many research psychiatrists stress that the pleasure of grandchildren is often better appreciated than the children: 'The love is not necessarily more, or deeper, but it is *better*' – there being more time to savour that pleasure.

And savour it I hope grandfathers do – for they are statistically a privileged group of men who live long enough to see the third generation of their own family. Husbands are usually older than their wives, then die seven years earlier, so that many children never meet their grandfathers, which is sad for both generations.

If you are a grandfather or about to become one, you are fortunate, and if you play your role with appreciation of that good fortune and an understanding of your place in a child's life, there are few greater rewards. Many men are better at grandparenting than they were at parenting.

The responsibility of fatherhood lies heavily on young men establishing their careers, balancing household bills and school fees and perhaps helping aged parents. Once they are grandfathers, however, mortgages are often paid up, careers or pensions well established, families off their hands, and there is that precious commodity that children need – time – to give to the grandchildren that never seemed available for their own children.

Grandfather Bill, always rather a remote figure in his own children's lives, was once daunted by the thought of grandchildren and prone to disappearing when a cot or pram arrived for a long weekend. Now they are of school age he dotes on his four grandsons and spoils his granddaughter so often she pleads to stay with him *every* weekend. Lewis Mumford once wrote: 'Every generation revolts against its fathers and makes friends with its grandfathers' and certainly grandchildren seldom have other than kind words to say about 'the other man' in their lives. Grandchildren all seem to love stories of the 'old days' as they will inevitably classify your childhood no matter if it was before or after the Second World War. Your own sons may have groaned each time you mentioned 'the war' (not again, dad!) and sighed as you related visits to *your* grandparents, but your grandsons will ask repeatedly for your reminiscences. A ready-made audience; what more could a man ask? I remember my grandfather talking of the Boer War and could not believe that he had been alive during the period of my school history syllabus! Young grandchildren will feel the same admiration and astonishment for you, so here's a chance to embellish those 'I fought back the enemy single-handed' stories to your heart's content – your audience will be wide awake!

Two schoolboys spoke with real admiration for their grandfather who has a constant fund of stories, and often boast about him to their friends.

Grandpa had to lie about his age to get into both the Great Wars. He added on a couple of years to get into the 1914 war in time for the Battle on the Somme, then he dyed his hair as it was going grey in 1939 and he got sent to North Africa and fought in the desert during the Second World War.

The word grandfather does have an aura of nostalgia about it – a ring of old world charm and a promise of noteworthy characterization.

'A little old man with long, grey hair . . . his face deeply furrowed' described one of the most well-known grandfathers in literature, anxiously pottering in his dusty curiosity shop, cared for by his granddaughter, Little Nell.

We learned a great deal from Charles Dickens about the Victorian grandfathers. We saw (see Chapter 1) such men in their undisputed roles as head of the family. Many of us have faded, yellowing photographs of gentlemen in frock coats with tall hats in their hands, and arrogant, stern expressions on their whiskered, often jowly, faces. They may be our great, or great-great grandpapas, but were they so very old at the time of the photographs? Probably not; but their positions were clear-cut – they headed the family, and demanded respect.

Grandfather Jeremy, at 45, is achieving respect in his career today – his photographs show a slim man in shorts and tee-shirt, playing cricket on the beach, his grandson toddling around after him. 'I can't believe my daughter has a child of her own; I don't feel any different now from when she was born.'

Other grandparents of his generation say they hesitate to tell their colleagues at work of their new status. 'It sounds so old, I'm afraid I may get pushed aside,' said one high-flyer in the City. It's the old ageism theme creeping in again and perhaps grandfathers could play a practical role in helping to do away with the nonsense.

But what do these younger grandfathers think of their grandchildren? Their answers are as varied as the children:

I was overwhelmed when the first one was born.

I was happy for my wife, although strangely unmoved myself; it didn't seem to have anything to do with me.

One grandfather wrote wryly of his experience – emphasizing the different roles of grannies and granddads perhaps? 'My wife recently gave 'birth' to her first grandchild. Her daughter, I believe, was allowed to play a minor part in the event, but the son-in-law and I didn't even get "walk-on" parts.' But he very honestly continued: 'The new grandmother is thriving. . . . and I, meanwhile, am beginning to assert my rights and confess to spoiling the child a little.'

I suspect more than a little! Many grandchildren – young and not so young – confirm their grandfathers to be 'a soft touch' – no matter how small they consider their role in the family to be. 'Dad was livid when I dropped out of college, but grandpa was OK. He always supports me when I'm in trouble.' Grandfathers may not run in the glamour stakes, but I have met many who are quietly making the most of their new status. 'My three grandchildren make me feel I want to stay young. I find myself going to keep fit classes and trying not to have too many business lunches. I think the children are doing me good!'

I think grandfathers can do the whole family good during some of the difficult times in family life. In Chapter 2 we heard of grandmothers interfering and becoming too bossy – and after all, too many females trying to run a household *and* a new baby can be less than harmonious. Grandfather can often whisk gran away at a crucial moment – or perhaps take the older children out of the house – they may be as relieved as grandpa to get away from the screams and the nappies for a while.

During more serious crises, grandfathers can be extremely supportive. Talking with many of the grandparents who are experiencing separation from their grandchildren (see Chapter 6) I found it was often the grandfathers who were able to bear the brunt for their unhappy wives. They can, of course, aggravate a situation, even cause a family rift, in the same way as grandmothers can. But most are as disturbed as their wives following a family break-up, and as relentless in their endeavours to regain contact with 'lost' grandchildren. Many, including stepgrandfathers, have spent all their money on legal cases, and several have started their own self-help groups to support other grandparents with similar difficulties.

For many grandfathers, a child becomes a special joy when he or she becomes the son or daughter they never had themselves. Broadcaster Ludovic Kennedy remembers how his grandfather adored him. 'He spoiled me, as I was the son he had always longed for.'

H. E. Bates was another literary man who wrote poignantly of his grandfather: 'I grew up in my maternal grandfather's pocket, bonded in a great warm mutual affection, neither of us able in the other's eyes to do the slightest wrong. He greeted my birth with the words: *Capital! We've had enough o'gals.*'

As they get older, you can take the grandchildren away for weekends or holidays, and they will want outings that their parents are not able to give them. As I said in the last chapter, grandparents can be thoughtlessly selfish: taking a young boy to his first football match, for example, is a father's prerogative – so respect that. What about taking him to see where you work, or used to work if you are retired? Unless his father is in the same profession or business as you (and this is rare today), a child will be fascinated by an afternoon in a City office, on a car assembly line, in a newspaper office or wherever. 'My grandpa is a teacher/pilot/farmer' is more entertaining than 'Grandpa potters about in the garden' – even if he does have pottering days now and then!

Grandfathers do not normally enter into competition with their sons or sons-in-law in the way that grandmas are sometimes seen as bitter rivals to daughters. As Simone de Beauvoir wrote many years ago, 'a grandfather's concern is deep, loving and *un*complicated', so that the relationships are filled with warm feelings.

For some children, grandfather was, or is, their carer. Jenny's parents left her with her grandparents when she was born and when her grandmother died, Jenny lived with her grandfather:

> He was a real friend to me, and really listened to my problems. The only trouble was that when he sent me to school he never told me that all children had to go; I thought he was punishing me for something, and I didn't understand what I had done. I suppose a mother would have explained. But I loved him very much.

Another little girl I shall call Jill, was also left with her grandfather, but sadly the local social services decided he was too old to cope and she was placed with foster parents. 'I was heartbroken. Grandad was the only father I ever knew and the only person I could confide in. Until I was sixteen I was desperately lonely, then I was allowed to go back to him.'

So many children talk of their grandfathers in these terms – as someone reliable, safe, easy to talk with. Arthur, approaching his seventies, talks about the days when he used to be dressed up in his best clothes to visit his grandparents:

Grandfather had a maid to open the front door and we had to let her announce our arrival, even when we were very young. Real old-fashioned snobbery! Now, my grandchildren rush in with friends, never knock, and I love it! But I adored grandfather, for all his rigid ideas. When I failed my eleven plus he was extra good to me, never scolded like my father; he just found something to praise – which in my case was music. He had a positive attitude to life, unchanging. That made for security, someone I could always rely on. I hope I can achieve that for my grandchildren.

Someone to rely on. It's a comforting idea, isn't it? Part of the charm of our grandfathers.

I have not found any glamorous or racing-driver competitions for grandfather yet! Perhaps they sense that they are a comparatively rare species and intend to keep to themselves for fear of becoming endangered?

On a more serious note, I am certain grandfathers *do* appreciate their good fortune. One grandfather – well into his seventies, voiced his feelings and I am sure he is not alone: 'My grandmother was the radiant angel of my childhood . . . now my grandchildren are just the same. They are the part of my life that is most joyous, that gives me most pleasure.'

4

Grandparents' Role
in the Family

*One of their (grandparents') most important functions in
every known society is their reserve role: to act as substitutes
ready to step in when the parents are, for whatever reason,
not there.*

Michael Young

The only academic studies in Britain on grandparenthood seem
to concentrate on the nuclear family – and any that have included
grandparents, to have classified them under the heading of *social
problem*. Lost in sociological jargon, few ever asked a grandparent's opinion of their role or of their view of family
relationships.

The media have always tended to present this 'older generation' as: *little white-haired lady in rocking chair by the fire*, and
bumbling old man, both often figures of fun.

The sociologist Marion Crawford, trying to amend this
stereotyped portrayal, in 1981 wrote of grandmothers as: *busy,
bluerinsed working wives who run the Townswomen's Guild and
go to keep-fit classes*, and grandfathers as: *active DIY enthusiasts,
still working, but less interested in work than in the local football
team, holidays in Spain, and a good bit of water for fishing*.

Well, she may be nearer the mark, by avoiding the tendency to
treat the topic within the context of *old* rather than *middle* age.
But as we have seen, grandparents come in all shapes, sizes and
ages. So is it possible to research this ambiguous role? What have
the few professionals discovered?

Grandmother wisdom

The most important finding confirms that grandparenthood can
be an invaluable source of vitality in *old age*, and of enormous

value in mental deterioration. One therapist talks of *a profound connection between grandparenthood and mental health*.

Many suggest that doctors, family therapists and others could maximize the emotional benefits of grandparenthood by using grandchildren 'within treatment' among mentally ill patients. Also, they acknowledge that grandparents can be a vital factor in the wellbeing and development of children of divorced parents (see Chapter 6). And most admit that their findings are, in essence, statement of conventional *grandmother wisdom*.

Research in the United States suggests there are five dimensions to the role of grandparenthood:

- *Centrality*: being the degree to which grandparenthood is central to the lives of the grandparents.
- *Valued elder*: this dimension identifies the significance of a granny and/or grandad who can enable children to learn at first hand of life several decades earlier.
- *Immortality*: this is when grandchildren give a grandparent a sense of their own continuing life, that is, carrying on the family line.
- *Reinvolvement*: many parents say having grandchildren brings back their own childhood memories, as well as the days when *they* were the young parents.
- *Indulgence*: an easily recognizable, extremely prevalent dimension: 'Grandma and grandpa spoil the kids something rotten!'

Grandparents describe their role

How do grandparents themselves see their role? Talking to many, of all ages, they enjoy the role, which does not make them *feel* old, only *sound* old, and the children help them to feel young: 'We were always in close touch with all our family, and now there are grandchildren it's becoming an even larger family – lovely!'

Every grandparent has a different interpretation of his or her role in the family, but almost all feel a great emotional upsurge when the event actually takes place. Once news of a pregnancy is announced, it is usually greeted with pleasure, though the significance does not always sink in at once. The grandmother-to-be will begin knitting tiny garments, searching for suitable contributions: 'I'm sure I've kept your moses basket, dear, and would you like your playpen back? I've used it for my climbing tomatoes, but we can clean it up.' The female bustle, perhaps a feeling that she can be useful again, creeps in; whereas future grandfather is wondering how his son is going to cope with the extra financial responsibilities.

It is an individual happening, and to a widow or widower, an event of special meaning – of nostalgia and mixed emotions. One widow said: 'Having become aware of death so early in life, before my children were adult, the new baby produced a warm feeling I had not had since my husband died.'

To the single grandparent, missing the physical contact of love, the very natural need to cuddle and touch, a grandchild's love is heartwarmingly spontaneous: 'A small child suddenly appears and gives you a hug and a wet kiss and it is wonderful.'

Of course, the sharing of grandparenthood is lost, and as grandfather Jack says: 'Thrilled as I was with the first grandchild, I felt a deep sadness that my wife had missed out on this happiness.'

David, a grandfather of five, had a touching story to tell:

I was not that excited when my grandchildren began to come along. Somehow without my wife it seemed they were just rather noisy intrusions on my Sundays. Then one day my granddaughter came and smiled at me and there was my wife – all over again – the same brown eyes, the same wide mouth and a dimple on the right side. Suddenly it all made sense – this little girl was a part of us. If we had not loved each other this child would not be here now. It's quite a thought.

A grandparent's role in the 1990s is governed by many factors:

- With more mothers going out to work, many grandmothers are called in to care for preschool children.
- Unemployed grandmothers are often the principal caretakers of infants of single, teenaged mothers.

- If granny is working, sometimes she can *share* the problems of school-fetching, weekend shopping, etc.

So, having a grandchild means:

- Your family will live on into the future.
- You are given a second chance to be a better parent.
- You can enjoy helping the children (with school work/ playtime).
- Your grandchild may achieve the things you/your child did not.

Conversely, a grandchild may mean little to a grandparent – loss of interest sometimes arises through living great distances apart.

Comments on being a grandparent are lively and varied:

We had five kids, so I reckon we deserve lots of grandchildren.

I would feel rotten if I didn't help my daughter with the kids; it's my duty as her mother.

I don't want to interfere; I never visit unless I'm invited.

When you are a mother you do what you think is right; when a grandchild comes you can rectify things you did wrong.

I feel sorry for people with no grandchildren – I mean, it's only natural, isn't it?

Such diverse comments make us wonder if the sociologists, psychologists or gerontologists have anything to offer grandparents and their families as a result of their research. Perhaps not. But grandparents' own experiences are *proving* at least one of their professional conclusions: 'Children who never know, or become involved with, their grandparents, do lose out on an enriching relationship – which in turn can continue through future generations.'

The role often includes practical help. Grandfather is used as chauffeur to afternoon school activities; grandmother supplies extra reading lessons, or a meal before mum gets home.

Babysitting, holiday homes, havens of peace during family crises – all can be supplied by grandparents.

Grandparent access visits can be a vital factor in the wellbeing and development of children of divorced parents – often essential role-models for absent or missing mothers or fathers. And if all that sounds daunting, the average grandparent fills their role most ably just by *being there*. Do you remember Maurice Chevalier singing, 'I'm glad that I'm not young any more.' Did you ever listen to his words? They included *comfortable*, *contentment*, and *no more confusion* – all of which sounds extremely attractive. Maybe that's the secret of so many grandparents? That aura they achieve of contentment, of never changing, of always being there. Stability and security are mentioned in terms of finance, budgeting, and pensions. But real security – in terms of emotional comfort – is something a grandparent can supply for free, with no frightening repayments. And for the grandparents the interest rates are always rising.

Grandparents as principal carers

Their role as principal carers varies in every family. But in homes where grandparents are involved and appreciated, they quickly become indispensable. As one granny put it, 'I guess I act as first reserve for my family.' The professionals say there is still a need to study grandparental influence on young families. What they will discover is that, from a child's viewpoint, *my family* is the normal choice of carer.

Marie Joseph, a well-known and loved author, has written of her beloved grandmother in autobiography and in fiction:

My mother died when I was born, and my grandmother simply took over. Welfare workers today would argue that she was too old – and in fact she died when I was seven (in my bed as we slept together) but I wouldn't have missed those seven years for anything. She gave me a wonderful start to my life – *she was my family*.

Thomas Jones recalls his grandfather in much the same way:

My mum died and dad sent me to granddad. I remember arriving with a brown carrier bag with my nightclothes and a change of boots, two books and a packet of gingernuts. Somehow granddad coped. And I loved him, even though he didn't talk to me very much – I always felt safe in his house.

With a little bit of luck

You did not ask to be a grandparent (although many mothers I know are often pleading with career-minded daughters to confer the honour upon them before they are in their dotage), but neither is it a time to cash in on your seemingly elderly status.

In the past, grandmothers, and even some grandfathers, expected their children, especially their sons, to keep them in their retirement. The words of the old song 'With a little bit of luck they'll grow up and start supporting you,' sadly voiced the actual expectations of many parents. Today, with better pensions, and more importantly with different attitudes, they seldom make such demands. But there are still a few grandparents who do expect financial assistance – as their right. They forget that it is a time when their own children are struggling to feed and clothe their families, repay mortages, perhaps meet school fees; to be asked to hand out money to a parent is a terrific extra burden. I have known such demands ruin a young family's marriage. I wonder if these grandparents realize what unhappiness they are causing. Of course, if a son or daughter is earning a six-figure salary and the grandparents are living on state benefits, it would be cruel not to provide all the help they can – but in many circumstances it is too much to expect. Apart from anything else, if it upsets the marriage, it will affect the entire family and eventually endanger the rapport between the grandparents and grandchildren. Surely nothing is worth that risk?

Helping financially

Practical and emotional support from grandparents is usually given in abundance – unconditionally, and with a love and tolerance that ensures a young family all enjoy the childhood years to the full. Many grandparents would also like to help financially as far as they are able: 'We have retired, we have a tidy sum put by, and feel sorry for the youngsters – living costs are so high compared to our day.'

Depending on income, any financial help is always acceptable. Even if it only entails opening a bank or building society account for a newborn grandchild, it gives grandparents pleasure to be able to contribute to that child's future. Grandparents able to invest larger sums for a grandchild's education may be worried whether they will incur heavy taxation or inheritance problems for their families. It is essential to consult your personal financial adviser, and discuss the various ways in which you can help, and paying school fees is often an extremely wise and welcome idea. Until recently, many grandparents took out seven-year covenants for the children, but since 1988 the tax relief on these has ceased –so it is sensible to look for other means of helping. Schemes such as the Capital Plan, run by the investment house Save and Prosper, are a popular way to pay school fees through one or more lump-sum investments. This can be both tax and cost-efficient, offering an attractive, guaranteed return, whilst ensuring the cheques are paid to the school – a safe and simple investment. To put your mind completely at rest, it is wise to write your intentions into your will, specifying the child's name and that you would like that money spent on his/her education. This will ensure that the Plan continues in the event that you die before schooling starts. Of course, if the executors find you have overfunded (this *can* happen in spite of inflation, if a child's school is changed, or he/she decided on a career needing less outlay than originally planned) the money will be returned to the estate. At the time of writing, the annual inheritance tax exemption limit is £3000 for each person – so grandparents could each contribute this amount annually to a school fees capital plan without coming within the scope of inheritance tax. (Be careful – each must have an independent income; a husband cannot give it to his wife to give to the child.)

Grandparents' names

Gramps, gran'pa, papa, grandad, goffer, big daddy! what a range of names the children bring forth, and yet they are said with affection – and quietly grandfather enjoys them all.

Gran, nana, gran'ma, gaga, are all used as often as the conventional granny – I personally love the sound of the French *grandmère*. The modern idea of christian names works for some, although granny Mary and granny Joan is a compromise which works well where there are two grannies. My children call my mother Gan Gan – the first grandchild's attempt at the word granny. She was somewhat disenchanted with the name, until I discovered that Queen Mary was so called by *her* grandchildren, including our Queen. Gan Gan has not complained since. . . .

In times of trouble

So are we talking about a role of pleasure, without responsibilities attached? Generally speaking, yes. But there are times when it becomes a role of intense responsibility, of vital importance within a troubled family – you must never underestimate this.

One of the biggest contributions you can make to a family is to help and support your grandchild's *parents*. You may never have imagined, when you gave birth to your son or daughter 30 or 40 years ago, that you would be reaping such rich rewards during the later decades of your life – neither could you have foreseen the deep pain that you would suffer on their behalf all those years afterwards. But such is the nature of parenthood, and grandparenthood: it is for life. If you are young enough to understand, also old and wise enough to tolerate, their relationship problems, that is, the possibility that they are not married, that your grandchildren are now termed *extramarital* children – or that your daughter or son is married to a foreigner and their children speak a language you cannot understand – your loyalty will be vital. Such 'different' marriages, and non-marriages, can bring devastating problems for parents, with the result that grandparents can either be left out in the cold, losing all contact with their grandchildren; or they can become the only possible thread of stability in a child's life.

The parents' role

In many families, the grandparents are elderly – only one may be left – perhaps now in a nursing home. Their days of being able to help the parents with their children appear to be over. Nevertheless, middle-generation members could be urged to encourage their children to initiate ongoing, mutually satisfying contact with grandparents. Even young children can help grandparents to survive depression, loneliness, and feelings of uselessness. No, it is not using your children as unpaid carers, it is teaching them about family love and showing them the satisfaction to be derived from giving. Remember, even if grandma is old and frail, your children will not be seeing her as you do. You remember your young, laughing mother, not this shrivelled person with the ungracious manners and sharp tongue; but your child has accepted her as 'gran', who has a fund of stories, and enjoys hearing about school – the two may find a great source of mutual entertainment.

When grandparents live far away, parents have an important role to play in keeping contact for the two generations. Taping children's voices, taking photographs, sending a child's first drawings – all give grandparents immense pleasure compared with the small amount of time and trouble taken. For children who are allowed to speak on the telephone, and play their laboured piano or recorder pieces onto tapes, those grandparents become a real part of the family. 'I never saw my grandma until I was sixteen, but from her air-letters and phone calls I felt I knew her, and we became firm friends when she came to stay.'

The caring and concern of the parents is reflected in the caring attitudes of their children. When these are extended towards the older generation it creates a bond which in turn will reflect on the parents when *they* become 'the older generation'.

Left in charge

When the life of a family is shattered by the death of one of its members, or by the separation of the parents, it is often grandma who can help to sustain the stability of the home and be of the greatest comfort to the children.

The adults in a family are so wrapped up in their own grief, or their own ambivalent emotions, they often do not have the strength to step into the role of comforter to their children.

One family, thrown into tragic confusion by the death of the young mother, found their way again when grandma came to stay. Though heartbroken herself at the loss of her daughter, she kept repeating what a worthwhile life their mother had led, how much she loved them all, and how they must treasure and keep alive their memories. She told the youngest girl how like her mum she was: 'You have the same pretty eyes.' She explained to the eight-year-old boy that his musical talent came from his mum; and for the ten-year-old twins she brought old photos of their mother in her schooldays. 'You are all part of her, all growing up to be like her,' she said. That family survived, and have one of the most closely knit and happy homes I know.

Death of a grandchild

The most overwhelming tragedy is the death of a child. To a grandparent it is devastating, whether that child is a baby in arms, a toddler, a lively schoolchild, or a teenager on the threshold of adulthood. It is a time when you need every ounce of strength and love within you, for a grandparent will often be called in when grieving parents cannot cope with the siblings.

Grieving themselves, grandparents have a crucial role to play, yet it can be a therapeutic one for them and for the young family. Keeping a household running, advising on the formalities, knowing who to call in to help – grandpa and grandma can be an invaluable source of comfort.

Margaret Gerner, having suffered the loss of a young son, and her six-year-old grandson, wrote:

It is terribly painful to be a bereaved grandparent. Not only do we hurt because we have lost a precious grandchild, but we hurt because we see our own child desolate and there seems so little we can do to help them. It will be a gap in their family for ever.

She also points out that sometimes the grandparents are referred to as *the forgotten mourners*. Grandparents must be allowed to grieve – for their unconditional love for the child was something special, reciprocated in full by a trusting grandchild. The loss cannot be exactly that of the parent – theirs is the ultimate tragedy and they must never be expected to *get over it*. But grandparents feel an appalling survivor's guilt: 'It is wrong, not natural, this is not the right order of things. We should be the first in the family to die – not that little boy, not that tiny girl.'

I have known grandmothers, desperately trying to help their own child come to terms with such a loss, telling them to 'be brave' or to 'think of the other children', or even saying 'You'll soon feel better'. They won't. They have to be allowed to mourn, with their whole family around them – to cry with the other children, and to talk and talk and talk of the beloved child who has died.

I remember attending a tiny child's funeral – watching the small white coffin being lowered into the grave and wondering how any young parents can live through such a moment – when the husband and wife clasped each other firmly round their waists and hugged each other. This is what they, and their children need most of all. Comfort by warm, loving arms says so much more than meaningless platitudes.

Every family is different, every grandparent faces life's crises in their own way, and the wonderfully caring self-help organization *Compassionate Friends* always encourages families to be honest with each other and explain how *they* feel able to cope. Mother may want to talk, father may want to be silent, and grandfather may want to keep busy. I have known some grandparents who have to go away – they know their weeping presence is of no help. As Margaret Gerner confirms: 'You may well feel angry – lose all faith in your God, and rant and rage at a world in which such cruel things can happen to innocent children.'

Those who feel able to stay can help in practical ways – keeping the kitchen going, feeding the other children, shopping, dealing with phone calls and letters – anything that makes life a little more bearable. One girl who was six when her brother died aged only five, told me:

> Granny was wonderful. She was filled with sadness that Bobby had died and not her, and often cried; but when she took me in her arms I knew everything would be all right again. She never left me alone, and *she was there*.

Granny was there

We should look to one of the greatest tragedies of our time to see demonstrated the overwhelming love of grandparents. Caring surely reaches the ultimate in compassion from those grand-mothers – and their numbers are growing – who are looking after grandchildren who have been diagnosed HIV-positive. Their ability to love the children that no-one else wants – either following the death or desertion of their parents – is moving welfare organizations to deep admiration.

Many grandparents have taken such children into their care – knowing full well that they would have to suffer the death of the grandchild, following so soon after that of their own child.

There *are* caring homes and hospitals, but it is in granny's home that these children will find that real, unequivocal, unconditional love they all need in their short, tragic lives.

5

Great-Grandparents

*I never thought my own parents would still
be alive by the time I became a grandfather!*

The role of great-grandparent still has a ring of unreality about it
– of living well beyond the three-score years and ten, of
becoming a revered and possibly unique member of society.

'I feel as if I've stayed around beyond my sell-by date', said one
great-grandfather, and his wife sounded quite apologetic, 'I hope
we haven't outstayed our welcome?'

From the most famous of all great-grandmothers, our Queen
Mother, to the 100-year-old Mrs S who is still the matriarch of
her adoring family, great-grandparents appear to be more than
welcome. Prince Charles once said, 'Ever since I can remember
my grandmother has been a most wonderful example of fun,
laughter and warmth,' and I am sure that delightful lady's great-
grandchildren feel the same way. In fact, the youngest members
of a family are usually the ones who appreciate this three-
generation gap.

'What fun to have another generation to talk to,' said a
teenager trying to trace his family history. 'Think of having a
living branch of my family tree!'

Yes, families with three or four generations still around *are*
lucky – the sense of continuity they provide is perhaps not always
so happily appreciated – but the great-grandparents themselves
know how fortunate they are to have enough years to watch their
families grow and develop:

Living long enough to go to my granddaughter's wedding was a
great thrill, but getting to know her two children was an added
bonus. They really do seem another generation, quite
removed from my own childhood. I feel I am a living history
book.

That great-grandmother is 84, and thoroughly enjoying her new status. Her husband gets confused with all the children. 'I don't know if they are grand or great-grand youngsters,' he laughs. 'All I know is it makes me feel really ancient to be pushed into a fourth age!' But he has a twinkle in his eyes, and enjoys nothing better than visits from his 'great-grandlambs' as he calls them.

A great-grandfather was celebrating his 90th birthday recently and four generations of the family gathered to enjoy the party. After a large buffet lunch, at which 'great-gramps' refused to sit down, the family assembled for a photograph. As the cameras clicked, I saw the old man counting up the 60 or more relations standing around him. He turned to his wife, 88, and muttered: 'Look what we've done, love!' Of course, the family wit had to make a speech about 'going forth and multiplying'; but the couple were delighted, obviously proud of their family, and thankful they were still a living part of it.

Victor Hugo expressed the emotions many may feel but cannot put into words: 'When very, very old, becoming a grandfather means stepping back into the dawn.'

Other great-grandparents are not great in terms of age. Still in their sixties, Ted and Angela married in their teens and now their grandson has a baby girl. 'Can't believe it,' says Angela. 'I'm only just beginning to feel like a grandmother! *Great*-grandmother makes me think of little Red Riding Hood – I ought to be wearing a lace cap and take to my bed.'

Angela looks barely 60 and is teased mercilessly by her family, not least by her husband. 'You ought to pity *me*,' he says. 'Think of being married to a great-gran!'

Margaret remembers her great-gran who really did wear a lace cap.

That was before 1920 I think, and I was about eight years old, and I was rather afraid of great-nan as we called her. She would arrive at our house in a brougham [a single-horse, closed carriage] and would peer at us children through a lorgnette. I thought it was a magnifying glass 'all the better to see me with'. She always had a criticism however hard we tried to be good. 'Your hair is not brushed properly, child!' 'Why does your mother let you wear such short skirts?' To my brothers she was all smiles. 'What a pretty sailor collar.' 'You *do* shine your shoes nicely, dear.' If I'd heard of equality for women in those days, I'd have joined a march!

Remember Nicholas and his grandmother (Chapter 2) who had such a close relationship which extended to include Nicholas' bride? Now, with their first baby on the way, gran is as excited as they are. 'It's almost the same thrill as having my own babies. Maybe that sounds a bit over the top, but everything has begun to have a deeper meaning.' I asked her to explain:

> I've been through the doubting years, we all have them, and I've seen enough sorrows to lose faith a dozen times. But when you see a new birth, not just for yourself, but for your children, and then for their children – somehow you stop questioning and just *know* there's a purpose to all our lives.

Memories

Journals, fading sepia photographs and bundles of letters tied with ribbons – Victorian grandparents' homes were filled with memories. Will ours be the same for our grandchildren? We will have photographs, and possibly films and videos of family occasions, and tapes of young voices. But what of letters and journals?

A filofax with its tabulated data and alphabetically sorted friends, is not likely to be of the same interest to our descendants, and certainly not to historians. Telephone calls have sadly replaced personal correspondence – there are not even telegrams recording the more dramatic events in our lives. Those old bundles of letters – so hard to decipher – at least gave a flavour to the times in which they were written: 'Father left for the war and the parlourmaid gave in her notice,' is one of my favourite entries in a diary belonging to my husband's grandmother. Drawers filled with yellowing pictures of faces long forgotten are sad. I do plead with today's grandparents to put names and dates on their slides and photographs, so that the family are not left with dozens of anonymous brides, unidentified babies, and strangely similar school children in unflattering uniforms with fixed smiles on their scrubbed clean faces.

I have my grandmother's diary of the year in which I was born –and I shall treasure that. The entries are trivial – who she entertained to tea, who attended church, and where she spent her summer holiday – but it gives me a sense of 'belonging' that we all need. We also have my husband's grandmother's bible, in which grandpapa entered all their children as they were born – their dates of birth, names and christening days. Sadly, these include the dates of two infant deaths among the ten babies. Without that book my children would never know how many great uncles and aunts they had, or where they lived. Does it matter? Yes, I find it does. For a family who have travelled widely, had disrupted lives and several homes, and now live far away from their birth places, such background knowledge is comforting, gives them a feel of being part of an extended family.

For any grandchild wanting to trace back one or more branches of a family tree, such books are extremely helpful. It has taught me, and my children, to appreciate names and dates on inherited possessions. I always scribble a name on a photograph, a date on a newspaper cutting, or an age against a child's drawing.

Clothes are casually discarded nowadays – 'easycare' seems to mean 'easy to dispose of'. Grandparents are no longer identifiable by what they wear; the birth of a grandchild, or even a great-grandchild, does not necessitate black lace shawls for grandma or a second gold chain to his pocket watch for grandpapa.

I wonder how many families still boast a 'dressing-up' box? I recall finding my mother's satin wedding shoes, one with a tiny gold nail embedded in the heel, for luck she told me. This made her life before I was born so much more real than looking at her wedding photographs. There was also a trunk filled with wonderfully flowered, flowing evening dresses, my grandmother's elbow length white kid gloves with a silver button hook to fasten their tiny pearl buttons; and several 'bucket' hats of the twenties; all living history lessons, but to us children they provided hours of entertainment on wet afternoons.

Will our denim trousers and coloured tights provide the same amusement for our grandchildren as they delve into their dressing-up boxes? I think they may – so do start a small memory collection. If nothing else, your great-grandchildren can sell your levis as antiques. . . .

Nostalgia

What's all this reminiscing doing in a book that emphasizes antiageism (Chapter 1)? Should nostalgia have a place in our lives? I think it should – provided it never dominates. Actor Robert Morley put it well when he wrote on the pleasures of age:

Conjuring up the past is so satisfying, but constantly dwelling in the past is stultifying for the brain, and boring for the family. What is far more important is to have grandparents, or great-grandparents, who can be a vital part of a family, rather than a lavender-scented memory.

Keeping in touch with the grandchildren

Many children, however, only have lavender-scented memories – or a few faded snapshots – in place of the grandparents they have never known. Some, and this mainly includes grandfather, have died long before they were born. *Great*-grandparents are unheard of, with no-one around who even remembers their names. Others may be alive, but living miles, if not continents, away – some have been tragically cut off from all contact through family separations (see Chapter 6).

For such children, there is a gap, a loss, in their lives. In some families, this is not too noticeable, with aunts, uncles, cousins and in-laws, maybe stepfamilies, filling their homes with so many relatives that they are not deprived in any way of extraparental love and attention. But for others, where there are few relations around, it is a definite loss.

At the same time, there are countless elderly people with no *young* relations. Perhaps they had no children of their own, and have lost touch with brothers and sisters, and are left with no extended families at all. Many, like the King family, live overseas. Granny King, now a widow, misses her two daughters and seven grandchildren who live in Australia: 'At first I was heartbroken, a visit once every five years is not enough to keep a close relationship going with growing children, although we write regularly and they are marvellous at sending photographs.'

Tapes are a great way to break down long-distance barriers. 'Hearing my grandson's first words; listening to my grand-daughter's piano lesson; hearing the whole family singing Christmas carols, are the greatest treats for us,' say one couple who have not seen their Canadian family for nine years. 'We send them tapes too,' says grandfather Frank. 'Informal and impromptu recordings of my wife and I talking in the kitchen or chatting about the roses I'm planting. We find it a comfort to know they can hear us.'

Long-distance telephone calls are not the devastating luxury they once were, and bring families closer on many occasions. But nothing can ever take the place of a child running in and out of your home – or of a granny's lap to snuggle into.

Surrogate grandparents

When you are old, you feel like a grandfather to all small children.

Victor Hugo, *Les Miserables*

Happily, many families are filling empty gaps in their lives with 'surrogate' grandparents or grandchildren. Mr and Mrs Dean have a family in New Zealand they have never met, and their neighbours have four small children whose grandparents died before they were born. The Deans have become grandpa and grandma to the four children, and all of them are reaping the benefits: 'It makes us feel needed again; we can babysit, knit jumpers, mend bikes, and generally be of use. And to hear their young voices calling through the window to us on their way to and from school is just wonderful.'

The children are delighted too. 'Now we're the same as our friends at school who've got grandparents – it's great,' says Anna, aged seven.

Even where there is great sadness, following a grandparent's or a grandchild's death – mutual comfort can be found between grieving families able to help each other in this way.

Where there is heartbreak during or after a young family's divorce or estrangement (see Chapter 6) lonely grandparents have found a badly needed fulfilment in becoming surrogate grandmas and grandpas to child victims of their parents' problems.

With so many single parents today, there are plenty of 'vacancies' for kindly people with grandparenting skills. Skills? Well, I suppose these include an ability to love without criticism, to listen with your heart as well as your ears, to be a refuge in times of stress, and finding *time* to play. Do you qualify? Are there children in *your* neighbourhood without grandparents? I'm sure, for many people, such an arrangement could be well worth a try. Who knows, perhaps some entrepreneural third-ager will start a 'Rent-a-Granny or Grandpa' scheme . . .

6

Stepgrandparents

*I've got three grandfathers and four grandmothers, some of
them are step ones, I'm not sure which!*

Sam, aged seven

The complex relationships in which grandparents sometimes find
themselves – often with little warning – come about for several
reasons:

- Your son or daughter marries a partner who has children by a
  previous marriage. When your own child becomes a step-
  parent, you automatically become a step*grandparent*, whether
  you were a grandparent previously or not.
- As a widowed grandparent, you may remarry yourself, and
  find your new partner has grandchildren – making you an
  instant stepgrandparent as well as being a grandparent.
- If you divorce, then remarry, the same thing can happen.

So – you have new stepgrandchildren. How do you feel? Are
you thrilled, anxious, or indifferent? Perhaps you resent them,
or long to turn the clock back to what you see as happier days.
Whatever your feelings, stepgrandchildren need to be acknowledged. They will be looking desperately for love, acceptance
and understanding.

If you have no grandchildren of your own, you may have
dreams of becoming a stepgrandparent when your son or
daughter marries a partner with children. Or perhaps you are
about to marry someone who has grandchildren already, and are
imagining all will be cosy and happy. But many stepgrandparents
are disillusioned, and find their new situation overwhelmingly
difficult to handle.

Maybe your son has married a girl you do not really approve
of, or like. She has two children and you feel they are nowhere
near as attractive or well-behaved as your own grandchildren. If

you want to build up a good relationship, and to help those children and their parents, you will need a great deal of tactful understanding. The youngsters did not want their parents to split up any more than you did, and they certainly did not want another mum or dad. Remember that, in many cases, they are being burdened with three, occasionally four, sets of grandparents.

At the same time they have to accept strange children to live in their home, or they may be living in a new strange home themselves.

It is a bewildering situation for all three generations, and it takes time – many experts say as long as three years – for a new family to adjust and settle. All stepfamilies are born from loss, and many of them have not fully recovered before embarking on this enormous new undertaking. Even those who 'wanted' the divorce will have suffered feelings of failure, guilt, anxiety and sometimes bitterness. If, as a grandparent, you can offer sympathy and friendship to all the grandchildren, your own and stepgrandchildren, it will restore at least some of their confidence in adult relationships. Let the parents know that you wish to help – they really will need your support at this time and may hesitate to ask, especially if your son or daughter has lost custody of the children. You may be able to provide a neutral meeting-place for a divorcing couple, or for the children who are not quite sure where, or with whom, they are going to live. Impartial love and caring can do wonders for their self-assurance, and a whole new warmth may well creep into your contact with them.

Teenage children may resent you: 'Your family are horrid, we don't want them and we don't want you,' can be daunting to an already sorrowful grandparent and very small children may not want 'a strange new grandpa and grandma, we've got some, thank you'. Patience is the only answer here, hard as that may be at this time. But if you genuinely want to help, you will have to appreciate each member of the family is suffering as much as you are. Think of the anxious day-to-day decisions and altercations that the parents have to face. As one mother said: 'You can't please everybody all the time, someone's bound to get hurt.'

Missing your own grandchildren

It can be even harder to welcome your stepgrandchildren if you never see your own grandchildren. Granny Suzanne still feels great sadness that her son's divorce has meant that she never sees her grandchildren. 'I am actively discouraged from doing so,' she says bitterly. She is only one of many who are denied all contact with their own families (see Chapter 7). But Suzanne *has* found consolation in her stepgrandchildren. 'For a time I felt I was *only* a stepgrandmother, but now they accept me and we can bring each other comfort. After all, we are all innocent victims of their parents' problems.'

Suzanne has also found that she is able to help her son come to terms with having a new family. He found it hard to give time and love to his stepchildren while still missing his own youngsters, and granny's constant concern for them made him realize how much they needed his love and attention, and how much this concern is helping him in his new marriage.

Sometimes a stepgrandparent, usually a grandmother, can interfere rather than help. Maybe she thinks the new family is being badly brought up, and chooses to forget that their upbringing is *not* her responsibility. She would be far better to love the children as Suzanne does, without criticism – which would do much to relieve any tension in the family atmosphere.

By contrast, a stepgrandfather may not be interested in his stepgrandchildren. 'No point looking to see if they take after *our* side of the family,' he may say resentfully. But it is rather like adopting children – as they grow they *do* become like the family they live with. Their looks, basic talents, and personalities will stem from their biological parents and grandparents, especially if they are still in frequent contact; but they may well pick up traits of a stepparent's character, and observe how a parent and grandparent relate to each other; they will absorb the principles by which they live, and learn from their manners and morals – an extended family can have an influence on any child.

Divorce can be an isolating situation, as can widowhood, and children who have large families, despite the difficulties these may bring, are generally the lucky ones with the least serious psychological problems. I know several children who never knew their own grandfathers, who were thrilled when their grandmother brought one into their lives.

Family history brought to life

The feeling of shared history and past events is integral to the traditional image of growing up with our grandparents, seeing our parents become grandparents, and finally becoming grandparents, perhaps great-grandparents, ourselves. Yet there is no reason why some family history could not be learned and shared through photographs and reminiscences of family events. Stepgrandparents sometimes make wallcharts of the many family trees. 'Helping grandpa and nana with the charts', can become a real treat for many children. They all contribute photos and other memories of themselves growing up, birthdays and holidays, etc., and gradually come to know more about their extended relationships. When a new 'joint' baby is born, adding a *half*-brother or sister to the complex trees – that baby becomes a symbol of the joining of two families and his/her name will be added on *two* of the wallcharts.

Such activities can help any stepgrandparents to provide a source of continuity and stability for anxious parents and bewildered children who find themselves part of a new stepfamily.

Family celebrations such as birthdays, anniversaries and Christmas can become nightmares. Teenagers do not want to spend time with all the extra, new relations – they have their own friends. The 'other' grandparents will need to be visited, and it will not be easy as comparisons are made by the younger children. 'Our real gran always bakes us chocolate birthday cakes, why can't we have them here?'

Stepparents trying to sort it all out could well do with some help from grandparents. Perhaps you could take the children to celebrate their daddy's birthday away from their stepbrothers and sisters; or plan two parties – one at Christmas and one at New Year, so that you can divide some of the warring relations!

You may well be feeling like outlaws instead of inlaws, and no doubt your stepgrandchildren will be having similar feelings. Sometimes the two sets of outlaws make friends through this very feeling of not *quite* being members of the family.

Sometimes it is easier for those grandparents who live some distance away from the young stepfamily. Letters, phone calls, and regular visits, however infrequent, can keep up a good contact and provide at least a small amount of security for the children.

Betty finds this easier than being too near. 'I find seeing my grandchildren brings back too many memories of happy days that will never return.' She is one grandmother who has never quite accepted her daughter's divorce and remarriage. This is understandable – mothers suffer tremendously when their children suffer. Both grandmothers and grandfathers will be feeling the loss of the original family situation. They loved being part of it, were fond of their son-in-law, and find it as hard as the children do to come to terms with a new family. Older grandparents often find it hard to accept divorce, and to be expected to behave like storybook grandparents with smiling impartiality, may be too much.

In a step-household, competitiveness can build up. If grandparents make derogatory remarks about the ex-partner who is, after all, *still* the children's mother or father, they will add to those children's pain and bewilderment. Stepgrandparents have to learn to let their children lead their own lives, sort out their own affairs, and not criticize or condemn.

Romantic novelist Barbara Cartland, perhaps the best-known stepgrandmother in England (her daughter became stepmother to Lady Diana Spencer, now the Princess of Wales) has a definite view of a stepgrandparent's role: 'It is to be as charming as possible and there is no question of interfering in any way.'

I have also heard stepgrandparents grumbling over the sudden influx of grandchildren into their lives: 'It costs a lot now that the number of grandchildren has been doubled overnight. Instead of five gifts at Christmas it is ten, and ten birthdays – help! What shall I do?'

What shall I do?

This is one of many familiar cries. 'I am a stepgrandparent, so how do I behave? What do the kids call me?' 'Shall we keep right out of the way? After all, these kids are nothing to do with us.'

Questions pour out, and the best place to turn will be to other stepfamilies, many of whom may already be members of *Stepfamily*. This is a growing organization who are working energetically towards increasing public awareness and improving public acceptance of the stepfamily in our society. They have done a great deal towards changing attitudes, and in encouraging families to help each other. They offer experienced advice:

- *Let the grandchildren know how much you care about them.* This really means enjoying the children, and why not? Never let prejudice get in the way of loving a child.
- *Offer practical instead of financial support.* For example, grandpa could give a hand in the garden and grandma could make some of the clothes or teach the children to play the piano. I know one grandmother who is teaching her step-grandchildren to swim.
- *Treat the new parents as a couple.* This is a difficult idea for many grandparents who are missing a loved son-in-law or daughter-in-law. But the new partners need emotional support which in turn will reflect on their children's confidence.
- *Try to find mutual interests.* 'We used to go for picnics, but the stepchildren don't like the country.' So why worry? Take them to the cinema, or museums – there are many free outings and exhibitions for children in many towns.
- *Always let the parents know any arrangements you make with the children.*
- *Try to be fair.* That means including them *all* in any treats: 'I try to be fair and include the new stepchildren, but my own grandchildren get upset and say I don't love them so much any more.' There will be days when you feel you just cannot win! But, it is worth repeating, it all takes time, and a great deal of tact, during this settling-in period.

The natural grandparents

Sometimes I wonder if stepgrandparents give enough thought to the natural grandparents. They are the ones who often have to suffer in silence when a 'new' family tries to usurp their rightful position.

Mary's daughter died, leaving her husband Paul with three children of six, eight and nine. Mary's mother adored them all and moved into their home at Paul's request to look after them. Two years later Paul married Jeanette, and Mary felt slightly inhibited about staying in the household when her own child was no longer there. But Jeanette was a charming girl and is only taking over from granny Mary very slowly for the sake of the children. Paul is wonderfully loyal, and encourages her to see as much of them all as possible. They often stay with her, and she looks after them when Paul and Jeanette take holidays.

Mary's only worry is Jeanette's parents, the stepgrandparents, who assume they are now granny and granddad to her daughter's three children. They constantly turn up when Mary is there, and she has heard them telling the children that they must not go to granny Mary so often: 'We are your *real* grandparents now!'

When grandma and grandpa get divorced

The rising divorce rate has left few families unscathed. School teachers can no longer assume a pupil's family to be the traditional two (natural)-parent household. Children take it for granted that many of their friends have two homes; many have seen their parents' involvement in two, perhaps three, divorces.

Yet they still show surprise when their grandparents divorce. Parents do things like that, even brothers and sisters, but not grandparents!

However, statistics prove that many grandparents do separate later in life (about 12 000 people over the age of 60 get divorced each year in Britain). Maybe after retirement they find there is little holding them together; each may see the future with different eyes – one wanting to settle down in a country cottage, the other wanting to travel the world or start up a business.

It will take careful explaining, and patience on the part of the parents and grandparents, if they are not to upset too many lives. Patricia was nine when her grandfather left his wife and married a younger woman. Granny was left alone. 'I remember we were not allowed to mention grandpa's name in front of grandma and vice versa. It was all hushed up, a taboo subject.' In retrospect she and her brothers feel it would have been easier for them all if they had been allowed to talk naturally: 'We liked grandpa's new wife, and she never expected us to call her granny. But it was made more difficult by all the adults being oversensitive about it.'

Joan and her sister were teenagers when their grandparents divorced: 'They both remarried and the two partners tried to pretend they were new grandparents to us. We hated that.'

Remarriage and grandparents

When my widowed mother announced that she was getting married, my nine-year-old daughter said in astonishment: 'I didn't know grannies were ever in the engagement column!'

She was not the only person to show surprise, and yet it is not at all an unusual occurrence among divorced or widowed grandmothers, and it is a very usual happening amongst grandfathers.

One old-established marriage bureau in London have a large number of men and women on their books whose ages range from 50 to 70, with several men in their eighties – many of whom are grandparents or great-grandparents. Women are more reluctant to become clients, for several reasons. They know that there are far more widows than widowers, and that if they are over 60 their chances of finding a partner are slight. Most of the men want new partners at least ten years younger than themselves, although one great-grandfather of 88 says he would be happy with a new wife of any age! Others are more specific: one man of 65 is seeking a wife from 40 to 55, and another of 74 says he must find a lady under 68.

I heard of a grandfather who had a very supportive family, several children and nine grandchildren, but when his wife died he consulted an agency within a week to find a second wife. The bureau say this is not unusual among widowers and divorcees. The cynical may argue that such men need housekeepers, not wives, but they also need companionship and many lonely women welcome the offer of sincere friendship and support in their later years.

Sex after 50

Prejudices still abound when talking of sexual desires and/or problems of anyone over 50. As for grandparents enjoying such delights of the flesh – well! Younger members of a family often tend to be remarkably prudish about their parents', let alone their grandparents' sex life.

Age concern is one organization that has faced and explored such issues, understanding that those in retirement are sexually active and that their sexual problems often do need to be attended to in the same way as they would for younger people:

> There is nothing abnormal about an older person who enjoys a sex life. Older men may not achieve full sexual satisfaction as often as younger ones do, but in normal health their potency should be sufficient for the enjoyment of themselves and their partners. If this is no longer the case, something is wrong and help should be sought. The unwanted effects of drug treatment or excess alcohol are sometimes responsible. Operations such as prostatectomy can cause sexual difficulties, and these can also follow a major illness such as a heart attack. . . . In women, sexual problems can develop with the menopause. But for both partners it is essential that embarrassment does not prevent them from seeking help – for the commonest cause of impotence at all ages is anxiety.

Consulting your general practitioner often results in frustration. 'What else do you expect *at your age*?' has been asked of a 50-year-old by a young and inexperienced doctor. *Relate* can give, or direct you to, helpful advice, but the most useful source is *SPOD* (Sexual and Personal Relationships of the Disabled).

Being elderly is *not* a disability, but if one partner develops a disability – like arthritis, partial paralysis following a stroke, Parkinson's disease – these factors will not necessarily suppress libido, but make full sexual intercourse difficult if not painful. SPOD can arrange personal counselling – often in your home area.

A situation with many facets

Marriage in your third age is not all plain sailing. One lady was a bride for the first time at 56, and found the sudden plunge into stepparenthood *and* stepgrandparenthood was overwhelming: 'I always envied women with large families, but now that I have one I find myself rather lost. I think perhaps they resent me. They love their real gran.'

In time, that family came to accept the new gran, but it is seldom quite the same: 'Our real gran was always there, part of our childhood, we knew her as our babysitter, and she gave us a sort of second home. Stepgran is more like a sort of visitor.'

Remember, if you think your new home with your new wife is better than the old one, your grandchild may not. For any child who loved her grandparent who is now living a long way away, or has died, the introduction of a new nana or grandpa is not always welcome.

Conversely, one grandmother said that her youngest grandchild, aged seven, asked her the day after his grandpa's funeral: 'When are you going to get married again, grandma? I'd like to have a grandpa again.'

When a stepchild is adopted

If a stepchild is adopted by the stepparent, then the biological father is deprived of all involvement with that child, whose name is changed, and *the adoption is irrevocable*.

For grandparents, this can be very sad indeed. For when the claims of a biological parent are abolished, automatically those of the extended family, including the grandparents, are also abolished. For a child to lose his grandparents when his parents split up is unbearably painful, but to have to lose them for ever is heartbreaking.

In fact this step is rarely taken nowadays, except perhaps when a father has given up all claims to his child, or is unknown, or has been convicted of mental or physical abuse towards his family.

A more appropriate position, custodianship, is now available, which gives full responsibility to the stepparent in the sense of being able to make decisions about the children, and on their behalf. This can give a feeling of security to a stepparent by regularizing his relationship with the children; at the same time it is *not* an irrevocable order, does *not* exclude the non-custodial parent from contact with his children, and it still allows a child to retain his rights of inheritance and nationality. Custodianship is, however, not available to all stepparents, since children who have been subject to the jurisdiction of a divorce court are not normally eligible.

If grandparents are brought into such decisions, they would be well advised to seek advice from conciliation sources or family courts – when the children's welfare and wishes must be given priority.

7

Grandparents' Rights

Grandparents represent stability in an unstable world. But the sad fact is that very often they are not treated with the respect they deserve.

Michael Young

When you start talking about *rights* of grandparents, it sounds totally alien to all natural family ideas:

Of course grandpa can take the children out today.
Grandma *always* copes with the baby when I'm away.

In the natural day-to-day interchanges of family life it is hard to imagine how anyone can query the *right* of a grandparent to see his/her grandchildren. Sadly, there are a growing number of grandparents who not only never see the children, but do not have the *right*, legally, to contact them. 'Even my birthday cards to my six-year-old grandson are returned to me unopened.'

How can such tragedies come about?

Family life is not the uncomplicated two-parent home that it used to be in our grandparents' day. We have talked about geographical distances that divide extended families; we have also seen divorce, remarriage, unmarried mothers and mixed-race marriages. The strain on human relationships within any one of these situations can cause alienation of family members. Within stepfamilies the strains can be even greater: 'It's bad enough having your kids in my house. I don't want your parents as well!'

When children are placed in local authority care (and that can mean being with foster-parents or in a children's home, or back home, or with other relatives or friends), or have been made wards of court, tragic loss of family support can result.

Saddest of all, many relationships within 'normal' households are not always so tension-free as we may imagine them to be. It takes only a clash of personalities between say, a mother and daughter or father and son-in-law, to spark off bitter arguments, rivalry or jealousy, and finally total alienation.

Following these appalling family disputes, grandparents find themselves cut off from contact with their grandchildren, and many have had to seek legal advice. It is then that the real horror stories are heard: 'I never dreamed such a thing could happen to us. Our grandson was whisked away and we, his loving grandparents, were powerless to help him.'

Lisa Parkinson, widely respected coordinator of the first family conciliation service in the United Kingdom, appreciates how tragic this multiple loss of extended family members can be for everyone, especially loving grandparents:

> Although some grandparents can be interfering and can contribute to family tensions, they are generally an enormously important source of support to whom lonely and confused grandchildren can turn for comfort when their own parents are missing or preoccupied.

Do grandparents have any rights?

As the law stands at the time of writing, in England and Wales, grandparents do not have any automatic legal rights over their grandchildren – which includes the right to make or keep contact with them. It is the *parents* who have such rights. When family feuds occur, parents have the right to refuse to let the grandparents see or contact the children. And even when such feuds come within the jurisdiction of the courts, a grandparent's voice is seldom listened to.

Grandparents in action

One of the most tragic stories comes from loving grandparents whose son and daughter-in-law, and two grandchildren, were killed in an accident. Their one consolation was that they could look after the surviving child, aged three. But the social services heard their story, decided that granny Barbara was too old (at

61) to care for the child, and placed him with foster-parents. It took them nearly two years of legal struggling, at great cost emotionally and financially, before they finally achieved care of the little boy. Imagine the trauma for that toddler – taken away from the only people left alive in his family that he knew and loved.

A Surrey grandmother whose grandson is in care has another story of lengthy legal proceedings to gain access to her grandson. Her daughter is schizophrenic, and was only eighteen when her baby, Tim, was born. After his birth the young mother was obviously mentally disturbed, refusing to see *her* mother. Strangely, the social services assumed this meant that granny was unsuitable to look after the baby and put a care order on him. An endless series of foster homes resulted, with interim periods when granny bought and furnished homes for her daughter and Tim was allowed to be with his mother. One set of foster parents were cooperative and Tim spent many happy times with his grandparents. But the daughter's illness was typical, and her behaviour so erratic that Tim was eventually placed in a children's home for about a year. During that time he was allowed to visit granny, until one day a letter came from the local authority: 'Your grandson has gone to foster-parents, all access will now cease.' Granny was devastated. 'Cut off from my grandson in a two-line note!'

This was to be a long-term, possibly adoptive fostering. Granny sent Tim a letter telling him she and grandpa still loved him. Incredibly, at the court hearing the woman judge said: 'What a foolish thing to say to a child.' Then a psychiatrist, who had never met granny or grandpa, told the adoptive parents: 'This child does not remember his grandparents.' This was absurd and untrue.

Tim is now an intelligent boy of twelve and remembers how he spent at least half his childhood with his grandparents. Last Christmas he sent them a card and a photo of himself. His granny writes:

We accepted that Tim should remain with his foster-parents. We believe he can understand that he cannot live with his mummy because she is ill, and that he *can* cope with having two families. We do not think that he will be made insecure by contact with us. We want to go on providing the loving relationship he has always had with us, and the knowledge of his natural family which will be so important to him as he grows older.

One of the most bizarre cases of incomprehensible judgement is that told by a grandmother in Hampshire. Her daughter became pregnant at seventeen and gave birth to twins – a boy and a girl. She was so young that she and the babies lived with their grandmother for nearly four years. Then gran helped her find a home of her own, and soon afterwards the girl married. After two years the little girl twin was taken to a health centre for a routine injection and the doctor noticed bruise marks on her neck. 'Daddy hurt me!' was the child's explanation – meaning her stepfather. A young, newly qualified social worker was called in and he at once decided the girl must be taken from her home. When the court case came up gran was not allowed to attend, and the Judge gave custody to the *stepfather's parents*! The man himself was given a very light sentence.

Separated from her twin, her mother, her gran – the three other *innocent* members of her family – the child was eventually sent to foster-parents. Her mother is allowed to visit her *twice a year*. Meanwhile, gran has taken every possible legal step to maintain contact with the child, to no avail. Her gifts and cards, social workers' letters and affidavits, are all kept for the granddaughter to see 'when she is eighteen'.

Perhaps even more curious is the case of grandmother Claire:

My happily married daughter, although delicate, had twin boys who we adored, and visited as often as possible. Imagine our horror when we heard that one night the two babies were taken – screaming – from their beds on a place of safety order – simply on the grounds that my daughter had been taken ill and her husband was away working. What better place of safety could they have had than with us – loving, caring grand-parents? We wanted to rush to them but found (more horror) that we had no legal rights to do so, and that the babies were with a fostermother who had no idea they had been premature and needed special feeding and care! It took nine months before we could get the twins returned to their parents – only 'moments' before the social services were about to put them up for adoption.

No family rifts, no divorce, and yet a family could have their world turned upside down within hours. Happily, *Place of Safety Orders* are soon to be replaced by *Emergency Protection Orders* (only enforceable for 7–8 days).

And since August 1988, grandparents who can show 'substantial involvement' with a child can be made *parties* to the case when local authorities are applying to court for a care order. They can be legally represented in court. But beware – *substantially involved* can be defined in different ways by different authorities.

Adoption

There is something very wrong when a child can be permanently adopted without the family being consulted. One five-year-old was put into temporary foster care when his young mother was ill, and although she eventually recovered, the little boy was adopted. The child's grandfather was able to give practical support to the family by giving their story as much publicity as possible. Hopefully, such cases will make those in authority in Britain aware of the unnecessary suffering imposed on innocent children and their families. Certainly continuing pressure, including support from the European Court of Human Rights, is being reflected in the new Children Act 1989. At the time of writing, grandparents are *not* permitted to apply to be parties in adoption proceedings; but *this will change* when the Act is implemented (1991–92).

Legal advice

Legal advice *must* be sought for this and all legal problems such as: the distinction between custodianship and adoption; disputes over access; guardianship of minors; financial help; legal aid, etc. The issues involved are too complex, and too individual, to give any other than general guidelines.

Time was when grandparents were the accepted carers should anything happen to the parents, but stable, two-parent families can no longer be taken for granted. A divorced parent may, understandably, wish to make a complete break from the 'ex' side of the family – especially in remarriage. A grandparent may strongly disapprove of a son or daughter's divorce and new partner. Not easy situations. It is up to all the adults involved, not to let prejudice deprive a child of a loving family.

Care proceedings

Grandparents can apply to become parties in care proceedings when a local authority may be trying to remove children from their parents. However, as both the *Family Rights Group* and *Age Concern* point out, some social workers show more interest in the extended families of children, and welcome offers from grandparents to look after the children, far more readily than others.

Each case has to judged individually – social workers are naturally reluctant to hand over responsibility for a child – they must be assured the grandparents are willing to cooperate with them and with the child's natural parent(s). The Family Rights Group will be happy to advise families with children in care or those involved in child protection procedures, and *Parents Aid* publish continually updated booklets of questions and answers for all the family.

Child protection register

If children are placed on an area register, it means the case will have been, and will continue to be, considered at a child protection case conference. Many of the professionals involved (who may include health visitors, the police, social workers, teachers, NSPCC staff, etc.) meet to discuss what action is to be taken. They can all suggest plans for the child's future, but the social services department has the ultimate power to make decisions about access, that is, who may see or make contact with the child. If grandparents wish to be involved, they have to *write* to the chairperson beforehand and ask for their letter to be read aloud at the case conference. It is always wise to ask a solicitor or the *Grandparents' Federation* to help you compose your letter. It is rare for social services departments to invite grandparents to case conferences, unless they are going to be involved in caring for the child.

For granny Rachel, courts and access applications were unheard of when her son and his wife went through a bitter divorce. Her young daughter-in-law had custody of the children, but granny managed to sustain a happy relationship with them. Until, apparently because of her son's unpredictable behaviour which included threats to his ex-wife and violence towards his children, they were put on the child protection register. This meant that granny's friendship was suspected by the authorities (in case she should allow her son to contact his children). In fact, the social services threatened to take the children away from their mother if granny continued to let the children visit her. Naturally she complied, but was devastated. 'How can you explain to your grandchildren that you love them, but can never allow them into your home?'

The consequences of divorce

The majority of problems seem to stem from the break-up of marriages. Usually the daughter or son-in-law is so embittered against the ex-spouse that she/he wishes to cut off completely from the other side of the family. One grandmother said wistfully: 'There should never be ex-grandparents, any more than exparents – only ex-husbands and ex-wives.'

Not an easy message to get across within an acrimonious household. Mary Stott, the well-known writer on sociological issues, once wrote: 'The only battle worth winning following a custody battle between parents is the emotional stability of the child.' Children quickly sense an *un*loving atmosphere, and will eventually question how such antagonism came about. Often, it is a new member of a family who causes the friction. Mary, a lovely warm-hearted grandmother, looked after her unmarried daughter's baby until he was five years old: 'I loved him like one of my own.' Then her daughter married a man who not only insisted on taking the child to live with them, in the same town, but denied granny any contact: 'I see the child being pulled, crying, past my house. How can human beings behave in this way? My emotions run very deep when I see that bewildered little boy. After all, a child has no voice.'

Grandfather Miles tells a similar story:

After my son's divorce he was given liberal access to his children, and we saw them frequently. But when a stepfather appeared on the scene, access was increasingly denied. Any gesture on our part is ignored. We sought help from conciliation agencies, who arranged for the children at least to write to us – but this happened only once.

Some ex-daughters-in-law can be even more bitter and devious. Kate not only has custody of her only son, but is trying to retain more than her share of the marital home and its contents. She is, meanwhile, denying access to her child's father and grandparents. Now, with a new partner to give her support, she is trying to blackmail her ex-husband: 'If you do not let me have everything in the house, I will never let your mother see her grandson again.' As granny says: 'Nothing can force Kate, only her goodwill.'

Once the Children Act 1989 is implemented, grandparents will be allowed to ask for leave of the court to apply for reasonable contact, even if the parents do not approve, and the court will decide if such contact is in the child's best interests. Let us hope that enough goodwill can be instilled into families, and into family courts, so that a child's interests always come first.

Wardship

If a child is made a ward of court, that court assumes the position of parent to the child: it can make any order it thinks best for that child, and it can grant, increase, reduce or terminate access to grandparents, or award them care and control.

But grandmother Rosie has a warning for all families: After three years of marriage, her daughter-in-law disappeared with the two tiny children. Nine months later, Rosie heard that the young mother needed help and so she looked after the eldest child, aged three, for a week – when the mother phoned to say she wanted him back. This happened several times. The mother was obviously unable to cope and the child spent almost all his time with his grandmother. Eventually social workers stepped in and a case conference was called, to which the grandparents were not invited. Afterwards, unaware of what had taken place at the conference, they were advised by the senior social worker to make their grandson a ward of court, which they were able to do. However, the costs of the case were high and, unable to get legal aid, they are now seriously in debt.

Granny Rosie says: 'No-one warned us how much a barrister can cost, and child benefits do not go very far. Maybe other local authorities are more sympathetic, but it should not depend on the whims of individual social workers.'

Rosie's struggle is far from over, but at least she is able to ensure that her grandson is happy and safe, whereas grandmother Peggy knows that *her* six-year-old grandson is neither happy nor well cared for:

When my son divorced he remarried, and his ex-wife, though wildly unsuitable, with several men in her life, was given custody of our grandson. I had seen a great deal of him, but to our amazement we had to obtain legal help to be allowed access of two weekends a month. I use them to put a little sunshine into his life – a few happy memories. We read together, go on outings, I give of myself rather than stick him in front of TV as happens in his squalid home. When he leaves, he cries and tells us his stepfather locks him in his room and often serves his food on the floor. A six-year-old! I appealed to the health visitor who visits the new baby in the house, and was told: 'Yes, the home is disgraceful, but these children have a way of surviving.'

Many grandparents even find difficulty in obtaining information about their grandchildren once they are taken into care: 'We are not asking to see them, only to know if they are all right.' Grandpa Tom has applied to every known agency without being able to find out even if his grandchildren are alive or dead. An adviser to the Association of British Social Workers says that 'Of course grandparents should be told if their grandchildren are well.' However, even those in authority have to admit that human compassion cannot be instilled by policies, rules or legal decisions.

Happy endings

Despite the sad stories, it can be a young parent who holds her family together and allows her children to suffer as little as possible during a crisis.

One divorced husband, who made life unbearable for his ex-wife and children, was finally denied all access rights. However, in court, the young ex-wife, who trusted her mother-in-law, and knew how much her children loved their grandparents, said to the judge: 'I would have no objection to the children's father having access if it could take place *at his parents' home.*' The social worker in the case confirmed that the children were happy there and so the judge agreed. The young father still makes trouble at times, and yet their mother is willing to let her children spend a lot of time with their grandmother – it involves a journey but she knows 'grandparents are part of their lives, I cannot deny them that pleasure'.

It is an encouraging case for all grandparents. If they are seen to be 'part of the grandchildren's lives', and social workers and the judge understand that, this does happen. So often we only hear of the sad cases, the bitterness, the misunderstandings, the ignorance – all of which lead to years of heartbreak and isolation. When there is cooperation, and *the children are considered first*, then the best can be made of an unfortunate situation.

Families at war

Perhaps saddest of all, are cases where family quarrels grow into complete breaks: 'My daughter-in-law thought we gave more attention to the cousins and not enough to *her* children, so we are *never* allowed to see them.' A simple case of extreme jealousy – but it has caused years of anguish and family feuding. Grandfather, a gentle man, says: 'It is the children who are being sacrificed. What is this doing to them?'

Child abduction – tug-of-love

When children are abducted by either their natural father or mother and taken out of the country, the normal ways to seek contact are denied. There are a number of agencies to help: *International Social Services* (ISS) can be contacted immediately for advice; *Reunite*, a pressure group that mothers of abducted children all over Britain can join, will actively campaign on their behalf; the *Children's Legal Centre* issue many informative publications, and *Families Need Fathers* have further lists. It is wise to write to your MP or your Euro-MP if you know the child is in an EEC country.

If the child has been taken to a country that has implemented the European or Hague Convention on child abduction, it should be easier to retrieve the child. Contact the Lord Chancellor's Department for help and information about the Hague Convention.

Grandparents can lend great support to a son or daughter in this predicament. If the marriage is a mixed race one, resist strongly the temptation to say: 'I told you so!' and try to treat this as any other domestic squabble. But it all takes a great length of time, and a great deal of money, patience and fierce determination to achieve what should be a natural, taken-for-granted relationship.

From all the evidence heard within family traumas, two things stand out clearly: far more compassion needs to be intermingled into the role of social workers who sometimes hold the future of a child – and thus of a whole family – in their power. Second, parents contemplating divorce need caring, experienced counselling so that they understand they are divorcing *from each other* and not from their children, or necessarily from their extended families.

Where to seek help

Whatever your particular family problem, it is wise to: (1) consult a solicitor experienced in family/child Law (your local Citizens' Advice Bureau will help your choice); (2) write to one of the self-help organizations for grandparents; (3) contact a family counselling or conciliation group.

Looking to the future

None of us can foresee the future. Always make a will, and try to encourage your children to do the same as soon as they become parents. Discuss this together. Should they die before you, do they want, and do *you* want, to become the legal guardians of their children? If so, it is essential to get these wishes in writing. You would still be wise to seek legal advice if a tragedy occurred, as some local authorities are less ready than others to encourage and/or enable grandparents to care for young children (remember granny Barbara, p. 62). As the Children's Legal Centre point out: 'Guardianship could always be challenged in court.' However, written instructions are more likely to be taken seriously than what might be seen as 'emotional decisions' during a crisis.

If the parents of your grandchildren are not legally married, only the mother has the power to appoint a guardian in her will, unless the father has custody or partial rights and duties at the date of his death.

You can also leave diaries, letters, or specified gifts, together with your will, in the hands of a solicitor, or bank, so that any grandchild (especially one with whom you have lost contact) will know that their once kind and loving grandparents did not deliberately desert them, and certainly never stopped loving them.

Grandparents' organizations, media publicity, even government and legal recognition, will never achieve ideal family togetherness for all. The best we can hope for is that all family members, *for the sake of the children*, will become aware of the vital importance of keeping in touch with their extended families, especially grandparents.

8

Grandparents in Retirement

Old age is nothing but a bad habit, which a busy person has no time for.
                                                            Winston Churchill

Whatever the future holds for you as a grandparent, or a future grandparent, the important thing is to keep busy once you retire. I have heard it said that anything *un*used will atrophy – which the *Oxford English Dictionary* defines as 'wasting away for lack of use'. I have seen just this happen to those who sit around and let their limbs waste away – and the horrifying thought of the same happening to the brain makes me tackle crosswords with enthusiasm if a day passes with no stimulating mental work!

Everyone views their pending retirement differently. Some, being self-employed, or fortunate enough not to be forced into retirement until they choose, ignore the whole idea. A lively 87-year-old grandmother who has had a fulfilling career as an artist, said: 'My commissions grow in number as I grow in age – it's great fun and I shall *never* retire.'

Another grandfather says: 'I'm so afraid this will mean I am relegated to being *elderly* and treated with contempt rather than respect.' This can happen. An attractive, young-looking grand-mother, recently turned 60, phoned the DSS about her pension. She was answered curtly, told to wait, passed from one depart-ment to another. When she finally was asked her age, the tone changed. 'They spoke slowly, called me *dear*, explained every-thing in simple words and repeated all instructions twice. It was all I could do not to laugh. Were they so young that they considered a 60-year-old woman to be senile?' That lady, who has five children and eight grandchildren, has an MA Hons degree and is still tutoring postgraduates, as well as running her large home. 'I had heard that in the eyes of society the pensioner is another species,' she says, 'Now I know how true that is.'

No-one likes the label of *pensioner*, although are the various alternatives any better? *Senior citizen* has a bureaucratic ring; *marpies* (middle-aged retired people) is dreary; a media favourite is *woopies* (well-off older people); there are the enviable *jollies* (jetsetting oldies with lots of loot); and the vividly self-explanatory *wrinklies*.

Regardless of their age or circumstances, men and women can find an undreamed of joy in their retirement years through their grandchildren, whose company and uncritical love add a dimension to life that was scarcely possible in earlier, more crowded and stressful years. And retirement years are *not* the handful of uneventful years our grandparents experienced. Many research scientists firmly believe that we are on the frontiers of a dramatic increase in human lifespan. Continually updated statistics point in that direction: by 2001, we are assured, four million of us in Britain will be over 75 years old, and over one million over 85 years old. At the beginning of this century our life expectancy was around 45; by the beginning of the next, it will be over 90.

There are many who dread the idea. The vision of a nation of great-grandparents shuffling around long after their 'sell-by' dates is not a pleasant one. But medical experts have encouraging news: they believe that old age can be made 'less painful and unpleasant by identifying, preventing, treating or curing some of the diseases awaiting us in our final decades', so the *quality* of this promised longevity should be significantly improved.

The anthropologist Desmond Morris, researching into the secrets of longevity found that those who lead truly happy lives had one feature in common – they refused to accept retirement as a time of bland nostalgia. 'The long-lived scorn any talk of the good old days and concern themselves with an active present.' That is the secret – being concerned with what you *do*, not who you are, or were.

So – unlike our parents, let alone grandparents, we can now look forward to two or more decades of active life between the end of employment and the end of life. These certainly need not be years of illness, and so how, without the pressures of having to support a family, shall we fill them? With an endless round of gardening, or slumped in front of TV? Men, without a work schedule, can easily drift into inertia. Throughout the western world one tends to see white-haired men standing idly on street corners, outside pubs or on park benches. Meanwhile, where are the women? Still battling with domestic chores no doubt, and they may well grumble at 'no retirement for us' but the physical work does keep them active. As one doctor said, 'We are far more worried about men than women in retirement.'

Women are used to juggling with their multiple roles throughout their childbearing years, used to organizing complex family plans and therefore more flexible and able to adapt, whereas the transition is more difficult for men. Conversely, if women have remained out of the work force, and many are still home-based, their lives will not change radically. The old adage 'for better, for worse, but never for lunch' was often quoted 50 years ago. When father was presented with his gold watch and commuted for the last time, no-one ever thought to ask mother if *she* would like to retire. On the contrary, she had to face more shopping and cooking, and a dramatic loss of her five-day-week privacy. In a few homes, this remains the situation and it takes a strong-minded wife, an understanding husband, and a balanced mixture of humour and commonsense, for the marriage to survive.

Poor grandma – she needs a few feminist friends! She might also read an entertaining book suggesting '52 ways to stay happily married even tho' your husband is retired' (see Further Reading). Such lifestyles are on the decrease, however, with today's grandmas also having been out to work and well used to coping with lunch-hour shopping, and grandpa well trained to take his turn with the hoovering. Then there are the thousands of widowed or separated grandparents who would dearly *love* 'someone to lunch'.

Well, what are the choices for these retirement years? 'Retirement is all right if you've got plenty of money,' say many who never manage to fulfil the dreams they had of life after work. They are right – a great deal will depend on a family's financial situation. So let's talk about money matters for a moment.

Pensions

Retirement pensions

One-third of all pensioners in Britain still need to claim supplementary benefits in addition to their state pension – which means they are not among the *woopies* and *jollies* featured in the glossy magazines and TV travel programmes. So how can they enjoy their prolonged 'third age'?

The most innovative change in taxation rules for pensioners came in 1989 – namely, the abandonment of the earnings rule. Now men and women may earn an unlimited amount without any loss of the basic pension. To some this might sound as if the Government expects everyone to continue working – to struggle on into retirement still trying to earn a decent living, barely able to make ends meet. But many pensioners enjoy the stimulation of a working environment, the friendships and the sense of being useful and needed.

Personal pension contributions

Retirement does not only mean retirement from your *previous* employment. It can herald *new* employment, paid or voluntary – possibly a chance to embark on a new career.

James, a grandfather of twin boys, studied picture-framing when he was made redundant at 60, and is now setting up his own business. Celia, a 55-year-old grandmother, left her nursing job to become an adult education teacher of English to foreign students.

If you are in a similar earning situation (and check with a tax expert), you can reduce your tax by taking a personal pension contribution – the limits of which will be a percentage of your earnings. Your contribution entitles you to a pension for life which you can begin at any time up to the age of 74 years, 11 months. For an employee, a personal pension contribution is paid net of tax due; for the self-employed, they pay the gross amount but may reclaim this from the Inland Revenue.

Your home in retirement

One of the biggest decisions to come under finance in your plans will be that of where to live.

Staying at home

If you are a council tenant, you may not be sure if you retain security of tenure; or perhaps you are eligible for the *right to buy* scheme, including the 60 per cent discount after 30 years of tenancy. Your local Citizens' Advice Bureau will have information and Government leaflets to help your decisions.

You own your own home and want to stay put? If your health and finances allow this, why not? Don't listen to the pessimists who talk about 'not managing all those stairs in ten years' time', or 'How will you keep the garden going?' This applies especially if you are on your own. As one widow remarked; 'My husband only occupied half my bed and one dining-chair, so why do my family assume I need a tiny place now he's not here?'

Talking of tiny places, don't forget your grandchildren – granny and grandpa's home may have been the venue for all family get-togethers.

Like all decisions, it is a personal one. Take your time over every aspect, decide what *you* really want, check that it is a viable financial undertaking. (Can you apply for a rates/poll tax rebate? Will your pension cover the mortgage payments? Would a lodger boost your income?) Then enjoy yourself – there's no place like home.

Home income plans

There is one serious warning, confirmed by top financial planning consultants. You may be lured by the many income plans and reversion schemes suggesting that you 'use your home as capital'. The retired are being offered loans without annuities, to spend as they wish, and with the interest being 'rolled-up'. Based on the premise that house prices rise on a regular basis, these schemes contain a high level of risk and *must* be viewed with caution. As an independent consultant says: 'We regard this as a very dangerous arrangement and one which could result in the loss of your home.'

There is an alternative: you can sell part of your property for a cash sum, which naturally relates to your age(s). Your tenancy is totally assured and you can use the money for any purpose you wish. This type of plan often becomes a matter for discussion with a whole family – beneficiaries included – but it is still essential to seek *independent* financial and legal advice.

Sheltered housing

Someone once said that sounds like 'a ghetto for wrinklies' – but talk it over with a friend who has lived in such a place for a year or more. Find out all the facts. They can offer economical living and peace of mind for you and your family, and do not, as the name suggests, necessarily mean any loss of independence.

The type of accommodation varies. It may provide a village-type area of bungalows or flats in a garden setting, with only a call-bell to the resident warden for emergencies and a high level of security to differentiate your home from any other private dwelling. You pay rates, gas, electricity, and a service charge to cover the warden's services and any other communal facilities. There are also large houses where residents have a bedsitting room each, and are provided with one or two communal meals daily. It depends how much you value your independence, how physically able you are, and whether you simply do not like living alone. Many of these housing schemes provide extra-care houses should any residents become in need of constant attention/ nursing.

Moving house

To the country   So you have always dreamed of living in a country cottage, perhaps by the sea? The attractions are understandable: cheaper properties can be found out of commuting range of a big city; traffic is minimal; air is unpolluted and you can at last grow your own vegetables and keep chickens. But will you miss your friends and family? They will all troop down with their spades and buckets in the summer, but not when you are snowbound in January; village communities can be hard to break into for newcomers; public transport may be nonexistent if the car, or you, break down from time to time. I would never deter anyone from choosing their own home, but it is sensible to weigh up all the pros and cons – moving is a big and expensive undertaking.

To the city Grandparents Ted and Molly, both ex-commuters, made a move in a different direction. They sold their suburban semi and bought a London flat. London to *live* in is a different world from the one you hurry into, wrest a living from, and battle out of. This applies to any large city, and this gregarious pair thoroughly recommend their idea:

> We are in the heart of life, yet need not go near crowds during rush hours. We wander in beautiful parks and gardens, endless free museums and galleries, enjoy cheap lunchtime and Sunday concerts. Weekends are a joy. Friends and family love visiting to 'do' the theatres, and the grandchildren adore river trips or sightseeing tours. We are enjoying life to the full.

Granny flats

A 'granny flat' also has a grey, elderly ring about it (one grandfather calls his 'grandpa's pad'), but living together with a young family especially if gran or grandpa are widowed can work well. Granny can babysit, grandpa can help with school transport, the young are available should one of the family be temporarily ill – the whole arrangement can be mutually beneficial. But insist on complete privacy – no sharing kitchens and communal telephones if you want the scheme to last without family feuding!

Living abroad

You may choose to sell up and move overseas. Homes in the warmer climates of southern France, Spain or on a mediterranean island are heavily populated with British grandparents.

Experienced advisers *Help the Aged* and other similar organizations all stress that you should 'proceed with caution'. Spend prolonged holidays in the country of your choice; check on the inflation-proof benefits of your pension if living out of

Britain; look into health care insurance. Finally, take a deep breath and ensure you have sufficient spare cash to visit the grandchildren or pay for them to stay with you. No amount of sunshine will compensate for not seeing the new babies until they are school age, or the beloved toddler until she has forgotten grandma and grandpa.

If your grandchildren are living as far away as America, Australia or New Zealand, you may well be tempted to move near them. Again, it would be wise to holiday with them first. Do you really like their new lifestyle? Would your lives be completely bound up with family and would this suit you, and them, after several months? For those with sufficient money to travel back and forth every year or so the decision is not so hard; but if it means leaving the old country for good, then it will take a long time to make the right decision. Once made no regrets. The most important thing in the world is to find a lifestyle which causes enjoyment for yourself and others, and not to listen too hard to the professional anxiety-makers.

Who are the carers?

All this talk of being the 'older generation' may appear absurd to those retired people who are still looking after their own parents. And there are many retired couples who have great-grandma or grandpa living with them. You have always enjoyed their company, never found gran a burden or grandpa a bore. But now you are beginning to realize that all ideas of retirement being a new-found freedom do not amount to much when you are tied to the house. No hope of choosing to live by the sea or in sunny Spain for you.

Whatever else you do, never become martyrs. Self-pity is destructive and isolating, and will help neither you nor great-grandpa. Talk the whole situation over with him and find out all the options: home help and meals-on-wheels, and often a kindly neighbour, will leave some days free; short-term care in a local nursing home if he is frail will let you have short holidays. An increasing number of sources of help are run by local authorities, voluntary bodies or private firms. *Counsel and Care for the*

Elderly provide a comprehensive guide of what home care is available and where to seek financial help.

Pre-retirement

The thought of attending a course on pre-retirement made grandfather Peter laugh. 'The idea! Who doesn't know how to retire? It means not going to work any more.' But how was he going to cope with not going to work? Not very well, according to his wife, grandmother Catherine.

For the first week Peter enjoyed 'every day a Saturday'. But he missed his colleagues, his motivation, even his commuting. He baulked at the idea of further education and laughed at Catherine's suggestion to take up voluntary work. 'I'm not cut out for hospital visiting!' But he found he was not 'cut out' either for managing his pension, for organizing his leisure, and was a sitting target for unscrupulous advertisers who tempted him with plans to 'turn your home into money'.

Many large firms run in-house courses, and now several commercial organizations are offering pre-retirement training. All cover the many issues facing you at whatever age you retire – including finance, pensions, housing, diet and exercise, and most importantly, *attitudes* to retirement. Be wary of those run by finance houses who *may* be biased towards their private financial schemes. If you want independent advice and information, look for courses affiliated to the Pre-Retirement Association (PRA). To be found nationwide, and throughout the year, these courses and seminars are self-governing, self-financing, and autonomous – many manned by volunteers, including retired people.

Leisure time

Traditionally, retirement has always been looked forward to as a long-deserved rest from toil. 'I want to contemplate, to stand and stare,' is still not an unfamiliar remark, and why not? Having worked for upwards of 40 years you want to enjoy some leisure. And leisure is not only found in exotic overseas locations. There are many perks waiting in your own country once you throw away the old alarm clock: cheaper travel, off-peak holidays, as well as more time to spend with the grandchildren.

Everyone has their own idea of leisure. Many delight in being out of the bustle of the commercial world and seem genuinely glad at not having to compete with the young any more. Why not become a rocking-chair person if you wish? Let those who enjoy life in tracksuits get on with their early morning jogging. Whatever you choose must never become 'a way of passing the time'. The only answer to such sadly negative thinking being that 'time would have passed anyway'.

Ronald Blythe, that most perceptive of all writers on life in old age, once said that 'What the old want most of all . . . is to be wanted.' Surely having grandchildren can go a long way to fulfilling that want.

Grandparents Jo and Marge exchange their home every summer for three months with a family in France, Italy or Spain, and provide a base for their young families to come and go as they please, depending on the grandchildren's ages and school holidays. This is an inexpensive alternative to boarding houses or hotels, popular with the children and far more comfortable for their parents than holiday camps or caravans, and great fun for Jo and Marge who feel they are able to help their families with very little outlay – only the cost of their journey.

These different lifestyles do all depend on individual finances, and pressure on many budgets does increase after 'a certain age'. Worth looking out for are the many new, enterprising organizations, including shops and magazines, who offer unique benefits for the retired. Notable among these is the *050 Club*. This is not merely able to provide friendships for those in the 50+ age group, but also to give impartial advice on a wide range of topics – legal, domestic, financial – which is in no way patronizing, but rather boosting the myriad interests of anyone who has passed 'that golden half-century'.

A 39-year-old new grandmother said she 'can't wait to be old enough to reap all those benefits!' In another few yers, her choice of organizations and clubs will no doubt be even wider – third agers are definitely a group to be reckoned with in the twenty-first century.

Work after work

In the past, retirement has only been about leisure, which is absurd in many ways – because abandonment of employment often means loss of motivation, initiative, and in some extreme instances, a short cut to death: 'Grandpa watches TV all day; he doesn't play with us any more.'

Are the pre-retirement programmes failing? Not at all – for where they leave off, there are now many excellent organizations and individuals who are determined to make *work after work* an attractive proposition for those who do not necessarily need to supplement their retirement income.

An elderly great-grandfather clinging to his desk while the younger members of his firm are aching to fill his shoes conjures up a vivid picture – often featured in old movies. But this seldom happens today when executive can mean any man or woman from the age of 30 onwards.

So what happens to the middle-aged who retire either voluntarily or by tactful request? *REACH* (Retired Executives Action Clearing House), founded ten years ago, was set up 'to bring retired professionals from business, industry, the forces, the civil service, local government and other occupations to work, for expenses only, for voluntary organizations or community groups in the United Kingdom which need, but cannot afford, their specialist skills'.

Taking executive to mean any experienced, skilled or specialist worker – REACH has helped thousands of people to find worthwhile and enjoyable work. Mike, a teenager, told me about his grandfather:

> He had to retire at 57 from being a technical director of a power tools firm and was miserable, until he started working as the director of a charity for children. They told him they could not do without his management expertise and he is extremely happy – and looks years younger.

The depressing thought that 40 or 50 years of training and experience is going to waste is at the back of every retired executive's mind – and to know that this expertise can be of use, not necessarily to his old firm, but to some equally worthwhile organization, is a tremendous boost to his morale, which in turn can reflect on his/her whole family.

Eurolink Age

In Britain we have tended to think of the European Community in terms of remote members of Parliament, unconnected with our daily lives. For those over 60, who represent 19 per cent of the population in the Community, *Eurolink Age* is changing all that.

Formed in 1981 it is, basically, a network of organizations and individuals concerned in ensuring 'consideration of the interests of older people and ageing issues' within the European Community. Members are drawn from all twelve EC Member States, and include retired people's organizations, the non-governmental social welfare sector, politicians, trade unions and gerontologists. The secretariat is provided by *Age Concern England* who are deeply committed to the European dimension of their work, with their own Executive Secretary now working in Brussels.

Eurolink Age campaigns vigorously for elderly people to be high on the list of priorities within the EC's Social Charter, with a list of proposals designed to benefit all senior citizens.

Age Concern England can supply full details.

Further education

Many people still regard education as the prerogative of the young – even those in their late twenties are classified as 'mature' students, and Grants are handed out accordingly.

However, come autumn, enrolment at adult education classes includes over 50 per cent of retired people. The classes offered cover a wide range – from art appreciation and dressmaking to public speaking and navigation. Cookery and car maintenance are popular, as are language learning and exercise classes.

Other grandparents want more than a weekly class – often

embarked upon for companionship or to fill a few dreary winter evenings. They want a full-time commitment and the aim of a degree or diploma at the end.

The Open University

This has a growing number of older students – over 7 per cent are currently over 60, and the pass rate in all subjects for these students is high:

> My grandchildren laughed whe I told them I was studying physics and chemistry. But I was tired of the youngsters taking their knowledge for granted, whereas I had never heard of physics in my school. Now I not only know what it means, but I'm finding it fascinating.

The most quoted family to enrol was one whose grandmother, mother and granddaughter all graduated on the same day!

University of the Third Age

Grandmother Sally, retired from running a bookshop and always having regretted not going to university, wants to study 'really seriously, some academic subject', yet does not want to take exams. She, and more and more like her, have discovered the University of the Third Age (U3A), an important and growing movement in Britain. Peter Laslett of Trinity College, Cambridge, first brought the idea to Britain from France. It is not organized by universities, but by third agers themselves – a sort of mutual aid university – they provide their own resources.

Dianne Norton, Executive Secretary of U3A, gave a concise description of this stimulating University's name. She spoke of: 'Childhood as our first age; work (encompassing social and family responsibilities) as our second; retirement as our third.' U3A believe that an active third age can postpone the dreaded fourth age of dependency (and possibly senility).

Members I have met are far from senile – many have started their own groups, and the National Office will give you advice and support if you wish to do the same. U3A offers all types of educational, creative and leisure activities for anyone no longer in paid work. Philip, a retired stockbroker, was delighted to hear of U3A. 'It was my grandson's teacher who told me of a centre in my town – he heard me say I was interested in learning for its own sake.' His wife was diffident about joining: 'I don't know *how* to learn. I had a rather indifferent, non-academic schooling.' The local U3A soon helped her to discover her talents. 'I found a whole new dimension to learning – I never knew what research meant before.'

Everyone is encouraged to take an active part in his or her group, but members are free just to sit and listen if they wish. Self-programming is the key word. A grandfather explained: 'It's back to the basic theory behind university study – the very way they planned their courses in the middle ages – and it works.'

Education and the generation gap

It is through this renewed interest in education that the two-generation gap is being bridged by many grandparents.

Daphne enjoyed being a grandmother to Alice and Sarah, fetching them daily from their primary school and staying with them until their parents came home from work. She was not the sort to interfere, but was worried over the little girls' reading and spoke to their teacher who said she was 'desperate for help. No-one can hear 35 children read individually in one day, let alone in one hour.'

Daphne thought hard and then offered her help, not only to Alice and Sarah but to the whole class. When the head teacher saw that she was serious, extremely patient with the children, and willing to take guidance from the class teacher, he suggested she should come in three mornings a week. This was an individual effort, but more than one local community education service now run schemes on similar lines. U3A members have joined in some of these and the idea is growing.

Jane, whose grandson is now in a middle school, is able to offer one-to-one teaching in French and German and has 'learned to use the new language laboratory'. In turn, her pupils enjoy hearing her descriptions of life in Europe, and as one eleven-year-old said: 'You don't rush us, you have time to talk.'

Association of Retired Persons

Started in the United States, where the 'grey lobby' has a powerful voice, this Association is aiming to build its membership in Britain 'to enhance the *quality* and *purpose* of life, by harnessing the economic and social strength of older men and women'.

This is a dynamic, anti-ageist organization which appreciates that enhancing the *quality* of life does not mean providing meals-on-wheels and waist-high light switches; rather it is about achieving self-respect and a continued joy in living.

Many active grandparents may hesitate to join any group which throws them exclusively amongst their peers. 'We don't want to be taken out of society just because we have left the work force!' But once they hear that the main aim of the association is to change society's *attitude* to ageing, they understand that this is a worthwhile voice. Their Chairman, Robert Rose, says: 'Our basic premise is PEP – concern for the Practical, the Emotional, and the Political attitudes of the older generation.' They are already lobbying for a change in the age discrimination laws, and they also strongly support the cause of legal rights for grandparents.

Teenage – middle age – third age

More and more organizations, newspapers and magazines, travel and insurance companies, all geared to retired men and women, are proving public recognition of this powerful consumer group – the third agers. Significantly many of them, in the 1950s, were the first acknowledged group called *teenagers*, with unique consumer needs; and it has been suggested that if they bring to this new group, *third agers*, the same enthusiasm and vigour as they did four decades ago, grandparenthood will be an era to look forward to with excited anticipation.

What no grandparent wants is to be *told* what to do, when to retire, where and how to live. An idyllic picture of living in the warmth of a large family is often a misapprehension if not a wild fantasy. An anthropologist has written of life for elderly grandparents among an unsympathetic family as 'death-hastening'. In a country such as Britain, where there are pension and other practical aids, living independently could be, and often is, the first choice of many grandparents, even if it means living alone.

Cynthia is a great-grandmother now, but still insists she is happier alone. 'If I want to get up early, or eat supper at midnight, I can do so without horrified comments from the family. And if I collapse on the stairs that's my own fault and I've told them all not to feel guilty.'

Betty and William prefer to be right in the heart of their family. 'We keep to our own rooms if we want to, but we know the family worry less if they can keep an eye on us, and we help them by house-sitting when they are away. We sometimes squabble, but not seriously – the grandchildren keep us on our toes!'

A positive attitude

Different lives – different viewpoints – as there should be. Legislation for the elderly has to enter some spheres – but independent choice should be priority number one for those mentally able to make a choice at all. 'I've not lived to 86 to be told I can't make my own decisions any more,' great-grandpa Fred firmly asserts, and he speaks for thousands of his generation.

His wife, 84, has a needlework sampler above her bed: *Today is the first day of the rest of my life.* 'It may be a corny phrase, but it seems all the more apt now we've retired.'

She is right. It is not a bad phrase for retirement, is it? After all, you will probably have at least a third of your life left – why not live it to the full?

9

Death of a Grandparent

People sometimes think that they are saving children from unnecessary distress by keeping secret from them the seriousness of what is happening to the person they love and even by keeping them away from the bedside. This is usually a mistake.

Dr Colin Murray Parkes

When the relationship has been close – and we have seen how happy a bond this two-generation gap can create – then the grief of a grandparent's death is great for a child. This may be the first major bereavement in his life, and if the grandparent is fairly elderly it is an opportunity for the parents to introduce the subject of death.

Initially, a child will learn something of the consequences of a family death from his parents' grief reactions. Grief may seem a strong emotion for a small child, but it must be recognized, acknowledged, and allowed to take its time. Parents sometimes ignore their children, being too upset themselves at a parent's death; some even wait until after the funeral has taken place before telling them the news.

When a child confronts death for the first time he is often concerned about the possible death of his parents – he worries about being left alone. 'When are *you* going to die?' You must never deny that you *will* die, one day, but it is wise to answer: 'I don't know when, but not for a very, very long time.'

The adult members of a family must remember that children do not necessarily express their emotions in words. Changes in behaviour must be watched for, such as thumbsucking, bed-wetting, or temper tantrums in the younger children; lack of concentration, school-refusal or angry outbursts and irritability among adolescents. With some youngsters, there may be a period of silent withdrawal, which can be wrongly diagnosed as easy acceptance of what has happened.

'Wendy has taken grandfather's death very well; it doesn't seem to have affected her at all.' Wendy may be hiding her grief because she is unable to put it into words. She needs loving, patient *togetherness* with her family.

Whatever the circumstances, and however the children appear to be reacting, constant reassurances of love and security are essential, as is an openness in talking about granny or grandpa who is dying, or has died.

Attending the funeral

Whether children should attend a grandparent's funeral is a family's personal decision. Most paediatricians, child psychiatrist and family therapists are in favour of allowing them – even encouraging them – to be present. 'That way they accept the death, a vital first stage in the journey through grief, and they feel included in the family which is also important.'

Age will naturally come into this decision: a toddler can disturb the service, and if an older child is too distressed it would be foolish to force them to come along – that memory could well override all the happy ones.

Before attending, it is essential that the children are told what to expect – whether it is a burial or cremation – especially if they are unused to attending church services. Talk to them about churchyards, gravestones, cremation, what an undertaker does. Let them choose their own flowers for grandpa; where possible, children love to pick them from a garden or field; or to watch the florist create a posy and write their own message on the card of remembrance.

Before the funeral, explain that the clergyman will talk about grandpa and that 'no-one will mind if we cry'. Tell them that all grandpa's friends will come along, and that they will be thanking God for having let them know grandpa, as well as being sad because they miss his company. A favourite aunt or uncle, a familiar friend, can often be found to sit with the children at the service, thus relieving the older bereaved members of the family of worrying over the youngsters. They like to be included also if there's a wake, or even a 'Come back for a cup of tea.' Teenagers may grumble at this 'adult' occasion, but would have hated not to be invited to 'grandpa's last party'.

My paternal grandmother, in whose home I spent many happy childhood years, died when I was away at boarding school. My mother wrote me a ten-page letter giving a full, vivid description of the funeral, the service, the flowers, the guests, and the 'happy time we all had afterwards, which granny wanted us to enjoy'. I remember being slightly shocked – with a moral indignity only a twelve-year-old can feel – at everyone actually 'enjoying' my granny's funeral. But it taught me more than I realized at the time. I have my mother's letter still.

Quite often teenagers are the ones who offer to plant bulbs around the grave, or keep it swept in autumn and tended in summer. This need not be a solemn task, but one which helps them to remember grandpa. 'We sometimes take a picnic to the churchyard, and my sister takes her radio, and it's exciting when the plants come up each spring' (Charles, eleven).

Mrs S remembers wearing a thick black armband and a black velvet ribbon on her straw hat as she was firmly taken to her grandmother's funeral in 1901: 'I was taken into grandmother's front parlour where she was lying in an open coffin on the dining table. My uncle lifted me up and told me to "kiss grandmother goodbye".'

The little girl did as she was told, but today, nearly 90 years later, she remembers exactly how she felt. 'Grandmother's face was icy cold and I wanted to cover her up to keep warm. But when they did shut the coffin I felt as if I couldn't breath – no-one told me you don't need to breathe when you're dead.'

Children seem so all-knowing and wise, don't they? They may nod when you ask if they understand, and as adults we often assume they know quite simple things that we take for granted. I remember a little girl being taken to a skating rink for the first time. She was about eleven years old, very agile and a lovely dancer, yet she was strangely nervous at the rink. After several visits with her parents she still clung to the side rail, refusing to venture out to the centre, although she could manage well on her skates. One day they overheard her talking about the depth of the water under the rink; no-one had thought to tell the child that there was not a deep pool underneath the ice. Once she knew it was solid, she became the best skater in the family.

A six-year-old child was living with her grandparents, and went through tremendous agony of sadness when her parents took her home again. None of the adults had ever explained to the child that it was a temporary stay with her grandparents – she had no preparation for what could have been a happy change-over instead of a sudden trauma. So much unhappiness is caused by not *telling* a child everything that affects her little life.

In all circumstances, children do need clear explanations, and to have them repeated at frequent intervals – especially in times of stress. None of us absorb everything we should during such times. And a beloved grandparent's death *is* a time of severe stress for a child. Discussions need to be kept open over a long period of time, until a child has fully accepted the finality of the event. Adults take a long time before they can 'accept' death, so it is not surprising that this is a difficult hurdle for children – especially those who are very young.

Children's perceptions of death

Here again, age plays a large part, but a child's experience and intelligence, also the relationships within the family, all play a part – awareness that death is irrevocable comes gradually, and the difficult grasp of abstract concepts certainly does not come overnight.

Signs of sorrow can be seen, even in babies. Once they can recognize a familiar carer, that person's absence becomes a huge loss. From two to five years, a child learns about trust – mummy goes out, but she returns.

Somewhere in those years he hears the word death, and recognizes a dead bird or insect as 'not alive'. Between five and eight years a gradual awareness of the finality of death begins to dawn – but cannot possibly be fully understood.

A five-year-old went to his grandfather's funeral, told all his friends that he was sad as 'Gramps has died and gone to Heaven,' but when Christmas came along, he asked when Gramps was coming to help him decorate the tree. 'He always comes' was his wistful remark – and his mother realized that even after nearly a year, acceptance had not *quite* come for that little boy.

All children are essentially practical, particularly the five to nine-year-olds, and intensely *people*-orientated. Almost without exception, and even in households where religion plays no part, death means going to a happy place, probably in the sky.

Up to adolescence, all children are far more afraid of the separation from loved people than of death itself – even for themselves (see Chapter 4). Nick, aged nine when his grandmother died, had suffered the loss of his father the year before. Amidst all the grieving he took his mother's hand one night. 'Granny can look after Dad now, can't she?' Nick's mother, and also his sorrowing grandfather, found enormous comfort from that little boy. 'It was such a charming, spontaneous thought – his granny would be delighted.'

Remember that children's emotions are deep, and they are able sometimes to face events with a greater openness than adults.

Peter, aged seven, was sitting beside his mother as she drove him to school. His granny was in the back seat. 'When I have children, will you be their granny?' he asked his mother. When she said yes, she would, he turned to his grandmother and asked, 'Will you be dead by then?'

Granny smiled and said that, being in her sixties, she might well be; but was touched when after a short pause, the little boy added: 'Well, could I have a photo of you just in case, so I can show it to my children?'

Religious beliefs

Grandparents, if brought up in the early days of this century, sometimes forget that their rigid religious beliefs cannot always help the younger members of a family. Explanations including a description of 'God needing the dead parent to work in Heaven' may sometimes offer help to a young adult. But to a small child who wants his grandfather back here and now, it can encourage distrust, even hatred, of a God who has 'stolen' grandpa away. Whatever your religious beliefs or disbeliefs, share your thoughts and doubts with the children. It helps the children to feel included and yet not overwhelmed by dogmatic theories beyond their comprehension. Teenagers will be grateful for such conversations – they like to be asked what *their* feelings are, and to know you are not treating them as small children any more.

Such conversations often start up close friendships between the two generations, and as we saw in earlier chapters, many grandparents find it far easier to be tolerant with their grandchildren than they were with their own children. 'I know I am not responsible for them and am therefore less critical,' said grandma Pauline. 'Perhaps it's because I have more time to *listen* to them. I remember telling my own children to *ask me later*, or *don't say things like that* – simply because I was too busy. Now, I'm never shocked by their comments – especially over the larger, moral issues.'

Grandma Pauline ought to know. With five grandchildren, three of whom lost their mother as well as their grandparents in an accident, she had to be prepared for endless questions. 'How long does it take to become a skeleton?' 'Why doesn't God answer my prayers?' 'Will mum know that I'm growing taller?'

In time, depending on age and understanding, a child will query further, from the wide-eyed plea: 'Why can't we visit grandpa in heaven, we could use a space rocket!' to the school-leaver's bewildered: 'How can you expect us to believe in something no-one has ever seen?' Many a grandparent has been confronted by a young adult refuting all the old answers. 'It's no use, grandpa, I *know* there isn't a God, and scientists can *prove* there isn't a heaven.'

It is always better to say, 'I don't know', while showing the younger person that you love him, and telling him how much grandpa loved him – rather than supplying quasi-theological theories that you do not really believe or understand yourself.

Always be honest – so important when dealing with children. I have heard grandmothers, no doubt well intentioned, explaining that 'death is only like going to sleep, darling', and giving a child a fear of bedtime for many years.

Visiting the sick and dying

We can learn a great deal from those who work in hospices, where the ethos of 'death being part of life' is shared not only with their seriously ill and dying patients, but with those patients' families. They actively encourage children of all ages to visit; to play with the nurses, with other families, to ask questions and to discuss their feelings amongst themselves.

One mother was anxious that her little girl of nine should not see her grandfather who was dying. 'He's so white and skeleton-like, with his sadly unseeing eyes.'

But the child, after the first visit, talked about 'grandpa's fingers feeling my face to see if I was like my sister. It was fun telling him about things – he asked me the colours of all the walls and the nurses' dresses and we played all sorts of guessing games.'

At one hospice I talked with a group of teenagers – all of whom had seen a parent or grandparent die. They are usually the most reluctant visitors to any such place, but here there was a specially arranged meeting place for them all, whenever they wished: 'It was wonderful knowing that someone else had the same feelings as I did when their granny died. I thought it was only me who was shy to tell my friends at school about it.'

Another time I saw a schoolgirl whose grandfather had died, playing carpet bowls in a hospice lounge with a grandmother whose husband was dying – both unconsciously consoling the other.

Keeping memories alive

If you are a surviving grandparent, having chattering children around you may be distressing, but it can also be of great comfort. Trying to help them can be of great help to you. Grandmother Joanna, whose husband died very suddenly, was endlessly greatful to her two grandsons, who rushed home from school each day to tell her jokes. 'We know you won't be able to cry if you're laughing, granny,' said Jamie, aged ten. Joanna was able to help the two children also, by giving them little tasks around her house 'that grandpa used to do'. They watered the window boxes, and dried the dishes and posted the letters and bought the morning papers.

It was all about keeping memories alive, a vital part of the grieving process for young and old. In time, granny gave eight-year-old Pete a set of books that grandpa had always read to him, and for Jamie there was grandpa's fountain pen.

Positive attitudes and explanations

At the same time, the parents were able to open discussions on the subject. Faced with challenges such as: 'How come grandpa's buried deep down when you say he's gone to heaven?' their mother used the analogy of grandpa's old jacket which he always used to wear in the garden. 'His body was rather like that worn out old coat. Remember how he used to complain of his stiff fingers and aching back? Well, he's left that behind for us to bury, just like his old jacket.'

One of the most beautiful explanations of death is contained in the old fable of the waterbugs and dragonflies. It compares a waterbug's short life under water with man's short time on earth, and its emergence as a beautiful dragonfly (unable now to dive back under the water to tell his friends about his new life in the sunshine) with man's life after death. Young children can easily interpret this idea of leaving the old body behind – of never coming back. I have often recommended Doris Stickney's booklet which tells the fable in a delightful story, and have found that parents and grandparents are also moved by it (see Further Reading).

Today, in the 1990s, death is not the taboo subject it was a few decades ago – but it is still dismissed as morbid, depressing and unnecessary to bring into family or schoolroom discussions by a large number of parents, grandparents and teachers. However, it has been proved, time and time again, that the homes where questions are answered truthfully, where a child knows that the adults in his life are easy to talk to, and receptive to confidences and problems, are the ones that offer the greatest comfort when a tragedy occurs.

10

Grandchildren Have Their Say

When I grow up, I want to be a grandpa.
William, aged three

Five, six and seven-year-olds

'Grandparents are your mum's mummy and daddy or your dad's daddy and mummy.'

'A granny is your mum's mum or your dad's mum. She is married to your grandad.'

'My gran and gramps are mummy's parents and they spoil us all. Daddy's parents are nice as well, and buy us loads and loads of presents.'

'My mum's dad is dead and my dad's mum is dead. My dad's dad lives with a lady called Molly. Molly is really fun to have around. They are not married.'

'My grandparents are very fond of me, they enjoy picking me up from school. They like gardening and enjoy pulling up dead plants.'

'My daddy's daddy can't hear properly so he has to have ear things in his ears. He is very old and he does not live with my daddy's mummy who has a bad leg. I don't know why they don't live together.'

'Grandparents are old and wrinkled and nice.'

'Some grandparents are miserable and don't give you back your footballs.'

'My mummy's parents have died and they are in heaven.'

'My daddy's mummy died before I was born, but she saw my mummy's bump that was me.'

'My grandparents get up at six o'clock in the morning to take the dogs for a walk, then they milk the cows and by that time everyone else wakes up.'

'My granny goes shopping, but my grandpa is brilliant at golf.'

'My granny lets me have my best sandwiches, but my mum does not.'

'My granny has a zimmer and lives in a flat; there is nothing very special about my granny.'

'Why do grannies live alone?'

'Nana won't let us play football in her garden. I expect she's nearly 100.'

'There is not much to tell about my grandfather. All I know is that he died in the war which is very sad. I think it was the war number two when there were bombs.'

'One grandmother lives next door and she buys us sweets on Saturday because Saturdays are our sweet days.'

'I don't know why granny lives in that big house with lots of other grandparents. It's sort of like a hotel but no-one goes home again.'

'Grandpa has no hair. He says he had some when he was at school – I wonder what he did with it.'

'I like great-grandpa, he has peppermints in his pocket.'

'My great-grandfather has his meals brought to him by a lady in a car, but when she's gone he gives it all to his dog. I like greatgrandfather.'

'Grans and grandpas are very useful, they buy sweets and toys and look after you when your mum is working.'

Middle school children

'Grannies think you're perfect when you're not. Your granny always spoils you when your mum's not looking.'

'I love my granny because she loves me and can keep a secret.'

'Lots of grannies have white hair, some dye it purple and some dye it the colour they had it before it went white.'

'Grannies are kind and happy and fairly old. They go to bed early.'

'My gran wears trainers and tracksuits.'

'I've never seen my grannies because one died of a disease and the other had a heart attack. If I did have a granny I would be really grateful.'

'My friend's gran is only 64. There's nothing up with her, she hasn't got a bad heart and can walk fine and she hasn't got many wrinkles. She treats me as if I were her granddaughter.'

'I don't like it when my grandmother talks. She says things once and then she repeats them about three times.'

'My nana always knows what's right, so when you have a worry you just go to her.'

'I love my nan because she does not smoke and gives me sweets. Her husband died and my mum burst out in tears and we'll never forget that day, and I'm sad he can't share these days with us.'

'What I do not like about my grandparents is they have split up and my grandpa does not give my nan any money.'

'I think my granddad is very nice, nearly every week he gives us 50p and a bar of chocolate.'

'When I go to stay at my nan's it's so boring because there is nothing to do around there and my nan has no pets.'

'Whenever I go to my nan and granddad's house they always say: "She has grown since the last time," and keep asking things when you are busy, like: "What did you do at school today?" That is annoying.'

'The only thing I don't like about my gran and grandad is that my grandad smokes and my gran smokes, but she hides it from my mum.'

'My grandad was in the war and he killed a lot of people and my grandmother was a nurse and saved a lot of lives.'

'My granddad is 71, but he is very active and does a paper round.'

'I dislike the way that three out of my four grandparents smoke.'

'I don't like my grandparents because they have got false teeth and my grandfather has got smelly feet.'

'If my mum says I can't have something, my nan goes back afterwards and buys it for me.'

'Nana just sits and stares at TV all day – she doesn't notice if we change the programme. But grandpa is my favourite, he makes me laugh.'

Teenagers

'My grandfather never talks to us. Mealtimes are awful; he sits silently, looking very fed up.'

'Granparents are different from parents, they don't know what life today is all about.'

'Both my grannies are OAPs, but one looks it and the other doesn't.'

'Nana always does the football pools and gets me to post her coupons and makes me promise not to tell mum and dad.'

'I meet grandpa in the pub once a week. He's great, we can talk about anything at all.'

'Mum never let us see granny and grandpa when she divorced dad, but we ring them up sometimes.'

'When dad died, grandpa came to live with us and he's very kind and takes us to school and helps mum, and gives us all driving lessons. But he says he wishes he could have died instead of dad.'

'Granny lives in this old people's home and we hate going there because it smells of old clothes and cabbage. When I get old I shall go and live in a tent.'

'My grandpa lives alone with his six cats and they make his house dirty, but he says they are better company than people. I don't think he likes us going to see him, but dad says we have to.'

'Gran and grandpa are always travelling round the world. It must be nice to be old and not have to go to work.'

'So long as I'm not getting into trouble, my parents don't want to know much more. But with my grandparents it is different. They want to know *much* more! All the details. What did you have to eat? Were you sitting next to a girl? They're looking back and thinking: "Once I was like that."'

Ronald Blythe

Recollections of childhood

'Grandmother always smelled of lavender water and grandfather smelled of pipe tobacco.'

'Grandparents meant Sunday. Granny cooked our dinner of roast beef and yorkshire pudding, baked apples and custard. We loved it all except that we had to take it in turns to say grace.'

'Sunday afternoons usually meant a long walk, then tea with granny. After tea she read to us, usually a fairy story, then we sang hymns.'

'She was a gutsy little lady, my grandma. I was only seven when she died, but I remember her rocking me on her knee, singing hymns in her clear flute-like voice, my head pressed against her cushiony bosoms which were encased in black serge during the week and black taffeta on Sundays . . . she filled my first seven years with such love that I grew up hardly noticing I was, in effect, an orphan.'

Marie Joseph

'I was scared of my grandfather; he would lock me in my room if I dared to be late for meals.'

'I knew that the children would be blessed and happy with their grandparents, supposing they were orphaned.'

Laurence Whistler

'Grandma insisted we visit her every morning while she sat in bed and said her prayers. If one of us giggled we had no breakfast. Hers was brought to her on a huge tray with a lace traycloth and she always had cream on her porridge, although we children had to have boiled milk on ours.'

'Of my grandparents, I remember my mother's mother best. Most of her time was spent reading novels: Jane Austen, Thackeray, Mrs Henry Wood, holding the book on top of a pair of combinations. If anyone came into the room, she would hastily whip the combinations over the book and pretend to be sewing.'

Jilly Cooper

'Of all my childhood memories, days spent in my grandparents' house are the happiest. I know now that they were poor, but to us they were rich – love, laughter, bedtime stories, cuddles by the fire, songs round the piano, hunks of bread and dripping on a cold morning – wealth indeed.'

Sources of Help and Information

Organizations of interest and support to grandparents

The National Family Trust

101 Queen Victoria Street, London EC4P 4EP
Tel: 0242 227187

Grandparents' Federation

78 Cook's Spinney, Harlow, Essex CM20 3BL
Tel: 0279 37145
Predominantly, but not exclusively, for grandparents who have grandchildren in care.

National Association of Grandparents

8 Kirkley Drive, Ashington, Northumbria NE63 9RD
Tel: 0670 817036
A conciliation and support service for all grandparents experiencing family problems. A 'Chatline' is open for members on Sundays.

Family Rights Group

The Print House, 18 Ashwin Street, London E8 3DL
Tel: 071 923 2628
The Group's legal advice for families includes a support network for grandparents of children in local authority care.

Parents Aid

Parents Aid Office, The Hare Street Family Centre, Harberts Road, Harlow, Essex CM19 4EU
Tel: 0279 452 166
Families with children in care helping each other. Local groups exist in a number of areas.

PAIN (Parents Against Injustice)

'Confers', 2 Pledgdon Green, Nr. Henham, Bishops Stortford, Herts CM22 6BN
Tel: 0279 850 545
Advice and help for parents whose children are on a Child Protection Register or in care.

Children Need Grandparents

2 Surrey Way, Laindon West, Basildon, Essex SS15 6PS
Tel: 0268 414 607
Small organization offering advice and assistance to grandparents who have been refused access to their grandchildren.

Newpin

Sutherland House, Sutherland Square, London SE17
Tel: 071 703 5271

Age Concern England

Bernard Sunley House, 60 Pitcairn Road, Mitcham, Surrey CR4 3LL
Tel: 081 640 5431
Provides training, research, information and helpful publications for use by retired people and those who work with them.

Help The Aged

St James's Walk, London EC1R 0BE
Tel: 071 253 0253
An organization to fund new ideas and help for elderly people in Britain and overseas. Their publication *The Time of Your Life* is an excellent handbook for retirement.

The Parent Network

44–46 Caversham Road, London NW5 2DS
Tel: 071 485 8535
Established to improve relationships between children and adults. *Parent-Link* groups run twelve-week courses locally to share experiences of family life and learn from each other.

National Council for One-Parent Families

255 Kentish Town Road, London NW5 2LX
Tel: 071 267 1361
Helpful information always available.

Divorce Conciliation and Advisory Service

38 Ebury Street, London SW1 0LU
Tel: 071 730 2422

The National Stepfamily Association
Chapel House,   18 Hatton Place
London,   EC1N 8RU
Tel: 0171-372-0844
Telephone counselling: 0171-209-2464

Pre-Retirement Association

19 Undine Street, Tooting, London SW17 8PP
Tel: 081 767 3225/6

Association of Retired Persons

Parnell House, Victoria, London SW1V 1LW
Tel: 081 895 8880

REACH (Retired Executives Action Clearing House)

89 Southwark Street, London SE1 Tel: 071 928 0452

Centre for Policy on Ageing

25–31 Ironmonger Row, London EC1V 3QP
Tel: 071 253 1787
Established to promote better services for older people; send sae
for full range of their publications.

SPOD (Sexual Problems of the Disabled)

286 Camden Road, London N7
Tel: 071 607 8851
Sympathetic counselling for the elderly.

Linkage

c/o CVS, 237 Pentonville Road, London N1 9NJ
Tel: 071 378 6601

University of the Third Age

National Office, 1 Stockwell Green, London SW9
Tel: 071 737 2541
For details of your local U3A send 6″×10″ sae.

050 Club

Greater London House, Hampstead Road, London NW1 7QQ
Tel: 071 388 3171

Eurolink Age

60, Pitcairn Road, Mitcham, Surrey CR4 3LL
Tel: 081 640 5431 Ext. 245

Further Reading

Burningham, John *Grandpa*. Jonathan Cape, 1984. For grandchildren and their grandparents.

Constanduros, Denis *My Grandfather*. BBC Books, 1989.

Exley, Richard and Helen (eds) *Grandmas & Grandpas*. Exley Publications, 1975. A book for the whole family to enjoy.

Hichens, Phoebe and Wilkerson, Joe *Marriage Round the Clock: 52 ways to stay happily married even tho' your husband's retired*. Quiller Press, 1989.

Kirby, Judy (supported by REACH) *Work After Work*. Quiller Press, 1984.

Manthorpe, Jill and Atherton, Celia *Grandparents' Rights*. Age Concern England and Family Rights Group, 1989.

Midwinter, Eric *Age is Opportunity: Education and Older People*. Centre for Policy on Ageing, 1982.

Stickney, Doris *Water Bugs and Dragonflies – explaining death to children*. A. R. Mowbray, 1984.

Whitfield, Richard (ed.) *Families Matter*. Marshall Pickering, 1987 (available from the National Family Trust).

Index